Maxx,
All the best!
Larry Barry

WHEN REALITY HITS

WHEN
REALITY
HITS

WHAT EMPLOYERS WANT RECENT
COLLEGE GRADUATES TO KNOW

NANCY BARRY

WHEN REALITY HITS
WHAT EMPLOYERS WANT RECENT COLLEGE GRADUATES TO KNOW

© 2007 Nancy Barry

Manufactured in the United States of America

For information, please contact:
Brown Books Publishing Group
16200 North Dallas Parkway, Suite 170
Dallas, Texas 75248
www.brownbooks.com
972-381-0009
A New Era in Publishing™

HB ISBN-13: 978-1-933285-87-0
HB ISBN-10: 1-933285-87-7

PB ISBN-13: 978-1-933285-88-7
PB ISBN-10: 1-933285-88-5

LCCN 2007924743
1 2 3 4 5 6 7 8 9 10

To my wonderful children, Chris and Lauren.

Your strong faith and passion for life inspire me.

TABLE OF CONTENTS

ACKNOWLEDGMENTS

---◆---

I feel as though this is the ultimate thank-you letter because there are so many people who helped me. I'll start with one big group hug for everyone who encouraged me along the way. You know who you are, and you know how much I love you.

A special thanks to the "dream team" at Brown Books Publishing Group. Milli Brown, thank you for being as excited about my book as I am. Your passion and enthusiasm for the work you do is contagious. My heartfelt thanks to Kathryn Grant, for taking me under your wing and holding my hand during the publishing process. You always made me feel as though I was the only author you were working with at the time.

To Janet Harris and Joy Dickinson Tipping, thank you for the time and attention you gave my manuscript during the editing process. I learned so much from you, and it was such a pleasure working with you. Thanks to Ted Ruybal for your awesome cover and interior design. And thanks to Cindy Birne for sharing your marketing and public relations expertise with me.

Every author needs a team of great editors, because two sets of eyes are always better than one. And I decided seven sets of eyes would be even better. In addition to the editing team at Brown Books, my heartfelt thanks to Bruce Tomaso, one of the toughest editors I know. Thanks for every word you changed and every mark you made on a page, because you made this book better. And thanks to Mary Beth Bardin and Jim Donovan, who together have over fifty years experience in the corporate world. I appreciate your editing the book from an employer's point of view. And to my twentysomething editors—Hilary Prine Baker, Chris Barry, Katie Donovan, and Kelly Oleson—thanks for editing from the reader's point of view.

Thanks to the amazing people I worked with at *The Dallas Morning News* and WFAA-TV, especially my colleagues on the community services team. You are the absolute best! We shared some great times over the years, and I am honored we had the opportunity to work together.

To Jan B. King, eWomenPublishingNetwork, thank you for planning and hosting an amazing conference that gave me a road map to navigate through the publishing process. Thanks to you, I met Christine Frank, who is the master of indexing.

And a special thanks to my dear friend, Debbie Mrazek, president of The Sales Company, for being a source of encouragement as we both wrote our first books. I'll always cherish our "power brainstorming sessions."

Thanks to my business associates across the country who took the time to complete my survey and/or be interviewed for my book. Your thoughts on the characteristics of a dream employee helped shape the chapters of the book.

To the members of my "Twentysomethings Advisory Board," thank you for sharing your thoughts and ideas with me, and being my sounding board.

Thanks to the "Fab Five," a fabulous group of recent college graduates who met with me as I was considering leaving the corporate world to focus on my passion of helping twentysomethings be successful in their careers. Hilary Prine Baker, Kari Dvorak, Stephanie Falls Wilson, Jamie Riddlebarger, and Natalie Ross, thank you for sharing your experiences with me as you entered the real world and started your careers. The information you shared confirmed I was on the right track.

Thanks to Karla Alfaro, Gaby Alfaro, and Katie Foster for the wonderful dinner we shared when we brainstormed the title of the book.

Thanks to Katie Donovan for choosing the promotion of *When Reality Hits* for your communications class project at Penn State. Thanks to you, Laura Finley, Kristen Karwatsky, and Sharon Mastrobuoni for developing some great ideas which became part of the master marketing plan.

My deep appreciation goes to my wonderful clients in my speaking business—corporations, universities and nonprofit organizations—who share my passion for helping recent college graduates be successful in their careers.

To my parents, Jean and John Boyle, thank you for your love and support. I owe you a tremendous amount of gratitude. Thanks to my late father for encouraging me to always do my best. And a heartfelt thanks to my mother for *everything* you have done for me.

To my precious ninety-seven-year-old grandmother, Bertha Wimberley, thank you for being one of my biggest cheerleaders. You are a remarkable woman.

And a very special thanks to our awesome God. Thank you for giving me the courage and strength to write this book, and leading me on this wonderful journey.

And most importantly, thanks to my wonderful children, Chris and Lauren. Being your mom is the greatest gift God has ever given me. I am so incredibly proud of you and deeply appreciate your love, encouragement, and support while I was writing *When Reality Hits*.

And a final thanks to the readers. Thank you for taking the time to read this book. I hope you enjoy reading it as much as I enjoyed writing it for you.

A Message from Your New Career Coach

—◆—

W hen I was in second grade, I knew where I wanted to work when I grew up. I wanted to work for the local electric utility company because my best friend's dad worked there. I thought Bill Aston hung the moon and wanted to work wherever he worked.

After I graduated from college, my childhood dream came true. I was offered a job at Dallas Power & Light and worked there for ten wonderful years. My plan was to stay there for my entire career, but I was recruited to join *The Dallas Morning News*. It was difficult to accept their offer because I loved my job so much, but it turned out to be the best career decision I ever made.

I joined *The Dallas Morning News* as community services manager. It was a dream job. Over the years, my responsibilities increased, and three years after I joined the company, I was promoted to vice president of community services. I was the youngest person ever to be an officer of the company. I was honored they had that much confidence in me, since I'd been with the company such a short time.

Several years later, I had the opportunity to take on the additional responsibility of heading up The Dallas Morning News Charities, an annual campaign to raise money for the hungry and homeless. While I loved every part of my job, this was the piece that truly touched my heart.

We eventually combined our community services department with that of our sister company, WFAA-TV. We moved our offices into the TV station, and my office was next door to the "green room" for the guests who appeared on our morning show. You never knew who you might have the opportunity to meet on any given day. I can honestly say I had the best job in the world. I worked with an amazing team at one of the best media companies anywhere.

After sixteen years, I decided to walk away from this dream job to pursue another passion. I had been speaking in public my entire career and absolutely loved it. I decided I wanted to start my own business and be a full-time motivational speaker.

One of my passions is helping recent college graduates go from the college world to the real world. I speak on college campuses and have clients who are hiring recent graduates. During my presentations, I talk about the topics covered in this book—the "soft skills"—that are so incredibly important to your success in life and in your career. I share what managers want you to know but don't have time to tell you.

I want this book to be a quick, fun, and comfortable read. I want you to feel as if I'm sitting right there with you in a coaching session. I'm your biggest champion, and we haven't even met. Hopefully, some day we will. As you're reading this book, I don't want you to think of me as someone who was a vice president for *The Dallas Morning News* and WFAA-TV. I'd like for you to think of me as your career coach, your mentor, or your new best friend.

When you think about your best friend, you think of someone you enjoy spending time with. Someone who tells you secrets. Someone who tells you what you need to hear, not necessarily what you want to hear. I'll be doing some of that. Some of what I cover will not be what you want to hear, but I promise this information will help you be successful in your career.

This book was written for recent college graduates with zero to five years' experience. If you're about to graduate from college, I encourage you to go ahead and read it now, so that when reality hits, you'll know what your future employer is looking for. After you get settled in your career, keep the book close by, in case you need a refresher course.

No matter where you are on your journey, I hope this information will help you succeed. I hope you enjoy reading this book as much as I enjoyed writing it for you.

Wishing you the best—always!

Nancy Barry

What's in It for You?

———— ◆ ————

You may wonder why you should read this book. After all, you just graduated with an awesome degree. You may think you already know everything you need to know. What I'll be sharing are things you didn't learn in college. No college course can completely prepare you for what you'll encounter in the workplace.

Employers across the country say many college graduates are not prepared for the real world. They say recent graduates lack important "soft skills," such as professional communication skills, business etiquette savvy, and a strong work ethic. They wonder if recent college grads understand the importance of building and nurturing relationships. And the list goes on. How can this be? You just spent four (or more) years getting a great education. Surely you're prepared by now.

Some topics in this book will confirm what you already know. A lot of them will be new. Some will be things you know instinctively, but I'll help you apply these soft skills to the work environment. You may have learned some of this material if you worked while you were in college or were involved in a lot of extracurricular activities. But even those experiences haven't completely prepared you to be successful in your career.

Some of what you'll read will make you think: "Are you kidding me? Someone actually said or did that?" They did. Some things I mention you will think are absolutely absurd. There are certain things about the workplace that will seem absurd, but it's reality.

Part of what I'll cover you learned from your parents, but unless you spend twenty-four hours a day, seven days a week with your parents to see them in action, you can't learn it all from them. And chances are good your parents aren't going to cover "Business Etiquette 101" or "The Importance of Building and Nurturing Relationships" over family dinner. (And I feel sure you're glad they don't.)

I'll include information that managers want you to know—and think you should already know. But until you're in the workplace experiencing these issues, you won't know. At this point in your life, you don't know what you don't know.

Are you ready—*really* ready—for the real world? You experienced a lot in college, but when reality hits, it's a whole new ball game. You've learned a lot, but you have so much more to learn. (I know that's not what you want to hear at this point in your life.) My goal is to shorten the learning curve. I'll share what I've learned along the way during my twenty-five year career, in an effort to get you off to a great start.

If you can look someone in the eye, have a good handshake, smile, have a positive attitude, meet deadlines, do what you say you're going to do, and be willing to make copies—you're halfway there. You may be thinking, "I'm *not* making copies. That's where I draw the line." Don't draw the line until you read why you'll want to be the one to make the copies. Just stay with me. I'll explain what's important to your success, and I'll do my best to explain why it's important.

You may not choose to do everything I recommend. Please just consider doing what I suggest. That's all I ask. The rest is up to you. I hope this book will help you understand what employers are looking for, and why your soft skills are so important.

They say you're not ready. After you read this book, you'll be ready. Remember, I'm on your team. I want you to be successful.

CHAPTER ONE

READY, SET, WORK

———————— ◆ ————————

O n your first day, you'll be excited and nervous at the same time. You'll wonder if you should have stayed in school and earned one more degree. You'll wonder if this is the right job for you. Those of you who have already started your careers know what I'm talking about. Let me tell you, you'll have these same feelings *every time* you start a new job, from now until the day you retire.

The First Ninety Days

Whether it's your first job out of college or one you'll take ten years from now, it takes about ninety days to get in your comfort zone. It takes time to meet the people, learn the culture, and find out who does what. Be patient. In those first ninety days, you may start thinking, "*What* made me think I could do this job?" You can do it, or they wouldn't have hired you.

1

When my friends at *The Dallas Morning News* recruited me to join the company, I was excited and nervous. I'd been with Dallas Power & Light for ten years, and it was all so comfortable. It took me three months to settle into my new position. It seemed like it would take forever to remember everyone's name. And it took me almost a week just to remember where the bathroom and copy machine were located.

There were many days when I thought, "*Why* did I think I could do this job?" I didn't know the newspaper business and wasn't sure I'd ever figure it all out. The only things I brought with me were my relationships in the community, which I soon realized were the most important piece of the job. Three months into the job, I was back in my comfort zone. I had gotten to know the people and the business. The other thing I realized in the first ninety days was how much fun it was to learn again.

As you begin your career, it will bring back memories of when you were a freshman in college. Remember when your parents dropped you off, and then drove off into the sunset? It was all new and a little scary, but you figured it out. Starting your first job will be the same. Give it those ninety days, and you'll be back in your comfort zone.

DID THEY REMEMBER YOU WERE STARTING WORK TODAY?

When you arrive at your job, hopefully, they'll be ready for you. In a perfect world, your desk will be clean, your business cards will be there, and your e-mail account will already be set up. However, the world is not always perfect. If your position has been open for a while, there's a chance they've been using your office as a temporary storage room. They may have forgotten your phone wasn't working. If things aren't quite the way you pictured them, don't take it personally. They are thrilled you've joined the team; they've just been crazy busy. Hopefully, your manager will take the time to give you a brief orientation and introduce you to the rest of the team. But chances are your boss is going to greet you and then run off to a series of meetings. If that happens, just find someone in the department to take you under his or her wing. They'll be honored you asked for help.

Depending on how busy your manager is, he or she may not have time to give you a lot of projects in your first couple of weeks. If assignments don't appear, ask some of the other folks in the department what you can do to help them. If they don't take you up on the offer immediately, it's not because they don't think you can do the work. They're just so covered up they can't slow down long enough to think about which project they could give you. Just continue to offer. One day, they'll think of something you could do to make their life easier.

While it may seem they forgot you were starting work today, they are thrilled you're there. Really!

Office Space

Decorate your office so you'll enjoy coming to work. Create a space you love, within company guidelines, of course. I have a friend who loves candles and decided she'd put a few in her office. Seemed like a good idea, until she set off the fire alarm. That's also when she learned that having candles was against company policy.

Your special touches in your office let people see your personal side. Just be sure it's not too personal. Think about this: Would you wear a skimpy swimsuit to an office pool party? Probably not. So you probably don't want to have a picture in your office of you in a skimpy swimsuit on a beach. Carefully choose the décor for your office, because it's a direct reflection of what you want your colleagues to know about you.

THE HOMEWORK CONTINUES

Think there won't be any more homework? Think again. I know the last thing you want to do right now is learn one more thing. You just spent years in college learning, learning, and learning some more.

You'll be learning for the rest of your life. (This one falls into the category of me being your "new best friend" and telling you things you *need* to hear, not what you *want* to hear.) The desire to learn something new every day is a wonderful attribute. Be like a sponge and soak up as much as you can.

You need to see the big picture. In order to do that, you need to understand the business. You learned a little bit about your organization during the interviewing process, and now it's time to *really* learn the business. Study the history of the organization. Understand its mission, goals, and core values. What's the chain of command? Get familiar with the organizational charts. What are the responsibilities of each department? How do they all work together?

Your job is important, but it's only one piece of the puzzle. You need to understand how your job fits into the big picture. You're part of a team, which is part of a department, which is part of the whole organization. If your company offers training programs, take advantage of them. If your company has a job-shadowing program, be the first one to raise your hand. It could be a fabulous opportunity for you to understand other parts of the company.

Research recent press releases sent out by your organization. Read trade publications. Get to know your competition. Get to know your clients' businesses. Get to know *all* of it. You'll be glad you did.

ASK LOTS OF QUESTIONS

Asking questions is how you learn. No one expects you to know everything. Successful people know when to admit they don't know the answer or how to do a specific task. A good leader asks lots of questions, sometimes to get thoughts and ideas, sometimes to get people to think in new and different ways, and sometimes because he doesn't know the answers and needs information.

Have you ever asked a question and as soon as you asked it, you knew the answer? It happens to everyone. So when you have a question, ask it out loud to yourself before you go running into your colleague's office. You might already know the answer.

If you're working on a project and you're not sure what needs to be done, ask questions before the situation turns into a crisis. And if you ask a question and you're not crystal clear on the answer, take a moment to clarify it. To be sure you understand something, you could ask:

"If I understand you correctly . . ."

"In other words, what I hear you saying is . . ."

"Let me make sure I understand what you're saying . . ."

Clarifying the information the first time will avoid your having to ask the question a second time. Be curious. Have the desire to know more. You won't know until you ask.

There's a Difference between Asking a Question and Challenging Someone

When you ask a question, be aware of the tone in your voice. It's all right to ask a question, but don't challenge your manager and her ability to lead the team. It's all in the delivery. Questioning or challenging someone's competence or judgment puts that person on the defensive.

Let's say you're working on a big project and you don't agree with the plan outlined by the manager. If you say, "Are you *sure* this is a good plan? I don't think there's any way we can do this," she is going to feel as though you are questioning her competence. Instead, ask, "Would it be possible to review the plan again to be sure we can meet your expectations?"

Can you feel the difference? Think before you speak. And always remember there's a big difference between asking a question and *questioning* someone in a challenging way.

Questions to Ask in Your First Week

After you've had a chance to settle into your new job, ask to meet with your boss. Tell her you'd like to meet to make sure you completely understand her expectations. Explain that you want to be sure you meet these expectations, and, hopefully, exceed them.

If people look at you as if you're crazy, it's only because you may be the first person who's ever done this. Here's what you'll want to ask your boss.

- In general terms, what are your expectations? (If you don't already have a copy of your job description, ask for one.)

- What's your preferred form of communication (in-person, e-mail, telephone)?

- How would you like me to keep you informed? Do you prefer detailed updates or bullet-point summaries?

- What drives you crazy? (So you can avoid doing it.)

- What's your management style?

- What can I do to make your life easier?

- A month from now, how will I know if I'm doing a good job?

Tell your boss you'd like to get up to speed as quickly as possible, so you'd love to have the following information, if you didn't already receive it in employee orientation:

- A brief history of the organization, its mission statement, and its goals.

- Organizational charts—so you can get to know people and understand how all the departments work together.

- A company directory. You're going to meet a lot of people in your first few months on the job. Every time you meet someone new, make a note in the directory.

- A list of members on the leadership team. In addition to names and titles, ask if there are photos you could review.

You may be wondering why you'd want to ask for photos of the leadership team. I am amazed by the number of employees who don't know who's leading the organization they work for. It's important you know their names and titles, but it's also important that you'd recognize your company's leaders if you saw them.

A friend tells a great story. Early in his career, he was riding on the elevator and saw someone he didn't know. When the other man introduced himself, my friend asked, "And what do you do?" The gentleman hesitated, then said, "I'm the president of the company."

The good news is that the president of the company was very nice about the whole thing. The bad news is that my friend was so embarrassed he almost quit his job. It's in your best interest to know who's leading your organization.

THE PEOPLE ARE THE MOST IMPORTANT PART

Years ago, I had the opportunity to work on an advertising campaign for *The Dallas Morning News*. Working on the "A World of Difference" campaign was an amazing experience. The local campaign was part of a national effort to expand cultural awareness and explore the value of diversity.

The ad campaign featured a beautiful array of people, young and old. The photo for the campaign was filled with vibrant color—the color of their clothes, their eyes, and their skin. The people you meet along the way will look like the people we featured in the ad campaign. I encourage you to get to know the people you work with; learn about their cultures and traditions. Learn about their backgrounds, passions, and visions. Ask about their families.

Even if you're busy, take a moment to show interest in your co-workers. It makes the workplace friendlier and will set the groundwork for developing strong relationships.

When we graduate from college and start our careers, many times we focus on the job title, salary, and benefits. But in reality, it's the people who are the most important aspects of any job. Take the time to get to know the leaders of the company. Get to know people in other departments. Get to know the cleaning crew. Get to know all of them. You spend a lot of time with the people you work with—cherish them.

Develop Relationships Before You Need Them

In order to be successful in your career, it's important to know how the entire organization operates. The best way to do that is to develop relationships with your co-workers. You never know when they might need you, and you never know when you might need them.

For example, if you're in sales, get to know the folks in product development, distribution, customer service, billing, etc. Make a list of all the departments involved in your clients' experiences with the company. Spend time getting to know the people in those departments, so you'll understand what your clients encounter when doing business with your company.

Many times people in sales are concerned only with closing the deal. Once the deal is done, they move on. You'll be more successful if you take the time to take a walk in your clients' shoes. Remember, it's all about them.

WHAT WE ALL HAVE IN COMMON

Throughout your career, you'll have the opportunity to work with people from all walks of life. It doesn't matter what position they hold, they're just people. Wonderful people—just like you. The one thing they all have in common is they are human beings. Treat everyone with respect. And I mean everyone.

When we were growing up, our parents taught us to respect people in authority. When you start your career, you'll automatically respect the people who lead the organizations you work for. After all, they're the ones who sign your paycheck. What about everyone else? Shouldn't we treat everyone with the same respect? If you want to be treated with respect, you need to treat others with respect. That includes the person who turns the lights on in the morning, the clerical staff who supports you, and the person who cleans the building at night.

Call everyone by name. Thank them when they do something for you. Choose to be the one who makes everyone in your organization feel special, no matter what job title he or she has.

WE'RE ALL ON THE SAME TEAM

Think you're alone? Think again. We're all on the same team. You aren't alone on this journey. You and your colleagues work for the same company, with the same customers and common goals. Some people get so focused on their own job responsibilities they forget they're part of a bigger team. You should be just as comfortable working in a team as you are flying solo. It's all about working together and getting along with one another.

Your success will be measured by your individual contribution as well as by the work done with, and through, others. You'll encounter a lot of different personalities along the way. Some people are soft-spoken, some are outspoken. Your success will be determined by your ability to work with *everyone*.

While the most important team is you and your boss, also look to the left and the right. Partnerships with your peers are key to your success. You're only as good as your team. Your team's capabilities will speak volumes about your own credibility and that of your organization.

A good team is made up of people who have different backgrounds, personalities, and ideas—all working together toward a common goal. Be glad. You wouldn't want to work with a bunch of clones. Your strengths will help the team. Their strengths will help you. That's what makes a great team.

Being a Team Player

Do you make it easy for people to work with you? Are you sincere, friendly, approachable, and helpful? When you express your ideas, do you do it in a respectful way? Do you celebrate the successes of your colleagues?

The people you work with are as important as the job you'll be doing. Helping others look good makes you look good. If the team wins, you win. You'll know you're a team player once you are doing the following:

- You put others' needs before your own.

- You're willing to do whatever it takes to help the team succeed.

- You use "we" ten times more often than you use "I."

- You communicate with the team on a regular basis.

- You know it's not about competing; it's about cooperating.

- You're open to their ideas.

- You support the team, no matter what.

- You roll up your sleeves to help, even if it means stuffing envelopes.

- You never ask anyone to do something you wouldn't do yourself.

IT'S ALL ABOUT THEM

The world does not revolve around you. It doesn't revolve around me, either. Making it all about them—your colleagues, boss, and clients—will help win their trust, support, respect, loyalty, and admiration.

When you're with someone, give him your undivided attention. Look him in the eye and make him feel as if you're the only two people in the world. Turn off those little voices in your head, and try to focus totally on the person you're with. Nothing makes a person feel more important than being acknowledged and listened to with genuine interest and without interruptions. Make a commitment to give others your full attention.

When Will It Be All About You?

When you live your life focused on others, it really *is* all about you. Listen to other peoples' needs, visions, and passions, and they'll remember how you made them feel. Bottom line, what they'll remember is *you*. So making it all about them ultimately makes it all about you.

Don't keep score. Give unconditionally. What you'll get in return will be amazing. Remember, it's all about "we," not about "me."

WHAT COMES FIRST—WORK OR LIFE?

The reality is that work owns a considerable part of our lives. But you can have *both* a successful career and a life. It's all about setting boundaries and maintaining a vision of what truly matters. It's easy to let your work take over your personal life, so it's important to be able to remove yourself mentally from your job when you leave the office. Be careful not to lose perspective on what's most important.

If you feel that you don't have a life anymore, keep notes on how you spend your time. Review the list and analyze what's getting the most time. Is it in line with your priorities? Is it in line with what you want to be known for? You'll always find time for what's most important to you.

Pace yourself. If you start working eighty hours a week, it's going to be real hard to go back to forty hours a week. Work hard, but be careful about the potential stress if you work all the time. You can run a marathon, but you can't run one every day.

Technology has changed the way we work. Thanks to cell phones, BlackBerries and e-mail, there's an expectation we should be available twenty-four hours a day, seven days a week. Once you start working all the time, your colleagues and clients will come to expect it.

Be a team player and be dedicated, but set limits for yourself. You can't go into the office on Monday refreshed and recharged if you spent the entire weekend working. There will be times when you *need* to work long hours; just don't do it day after day, week after week, year after year.

If you find you have to work long hours all the time, take a look at your workload and productivity level. Are you being as productive as you can be? Or is your job truly too much for one person to handle? If it's the latter, have a conversation with your boss. She wants you to be successful. She hired you because you were the best candidate for the position and doesn't want you to get burned out.

There may be days when you say, "I don't have a life!" Sure you do; you have a great life. It's just different from the great life you had in college.

CHAPTER TWO

WHEN REALITY HITS

here did the time go? Doesn't it seem as though you were just leaving to go to college? Your life was filled with excitement, and a little fear, as you left the comfort of your home.

Your freshman year took a little adjustment: new city, new friends, new professors, and new responsibilities. Then one day, it all started feeling comfortable. Your sophomore and junior years flew by. All of a sudden, you were a senior in college. By the spring of your senior year, reality hit. You weren't quite ready to graduate and enter the real world. So you started thinking about graduate school.

But no matter how many degrees you earn, at some point your college years will be over and you'll begin your career. Then it all starts over again: the excitement and the fear of the unknown. Never fear, your life will be great. You'll settle into a career, and you'll feel comfortable again. It'll just take time.

Your college years were some of the best years of your life. Now, the best is yet to come.

Starting a New Career Is Like Learning to Drive

Remember when you were finally old enough to learn how to drive? It was exciting and scary, all at the same time. Entering the real world will feel just the same.

When you started driving, you were on the road with a bunch of people you didn't know. Some were good drivers, some weren't. Some were young, some were old, and some were *really* old. The work world looks just the same. You'll be working with a bunch of new people. Some will be young like you, some will be old, and some will seem real old. After you have a chance to get to know them, work with them, and learn from them, you'll be back in your comfort zone.

When you got your first car, you had to learn how everything worked. How were you going to remember it all? It just took time. The same holds true in your career. You'll be joining an organization you know a little bit about. As you settle in, you'll learn more, such as how everyone works together toward a common goal. At first, you'll wonder if you'll ever figure it all out. You will.

The first week you had your car, it was spotless, shining like brand new. You had so much pride in your car. By week two, you still had pride in your car, but it started looking as if you lived in it.

When you start your career, you'll want to take pride in your professional appearance. Take pride in the great work you do. Take pride in knowing you have the ability to make a difference in the world.

Remember when you had your first accident; you thought the world was going to come to an end. You thought your parents were going to wring your neck. Seriously, they were disappointed you had a wreck, but all they really cared about was you. All that mattered was that you were not hurt.

When you make your first big mistake at work, it'll bring back memories of the day you had to call your parents about that accident. Making mistakes is a fact of life. We're human; making mistakes is how we learn. The world is not going to come to an end if you make a mistake in your career.

Getting your driver's license gave you independence. You were out on the road, all by yourself. That independence felt great but was also a little scary at times. Starting your career will feel much the same. You'll love the independence of having your own money and your own place to live, but there will be days when it'll seem scary.

You survived learning how to drive. You'll also survive launching your new career.

THE COLLEGE WORLD VERSUS THE REAL WORLD

Entering the real world will be a bit of a rude awakening. It's wonderful, but different from anything you've experienced before. I don't want to scare you. I just want you to be prepared. Your life will be different, but it has to be as you enter the next stage of your journey.

While you're in college, you're on your own. You've been your own boss. Now you have one. In college, you come and go as you please. Now you'll need to let other people know when you're coming and going. No more naps and you have to get up early every day. Your summers are gone, and your wardrobe changes.

And you'll quickly realize that no one loves you like your mom. Your boss isn't going to care if you stayed out late the night before. She'll expect you to be responsible and come to work on time, every day, ready to go.

WHAT EMPLOYERS WANT YOU TO KNOW

What do all college graduates have in common? A degree. So, what's going to separate you from the rest of the pack? What does an employer look for in addition to your degree?

Let's say I'm the hiring manager. We have an opening and have narrowed the field of candidates to four. All graduated with the same degree and the same GPA. How will I determine whom we'll hire? Throughout my twenty-five year career, I've always said if a candidate has a great attitude, is passionate, sees everything as an opportunity, has a good work ethic, and is energetic, enthusiastic, and dedicated—we can teach him or her to do anything.

If you look at any job description, you will see it lists the qualifications for the position. In addition to a degree and perhaps some years of experience, the rest of the description lists "soft skills." That's what I'll focus on in the chapters that follow. Here are some of those soft skills you'll see.

- Excellent verbal and written communication skills
- A commitment to exceptional customer service
- Sound judgment and business maturity
- Professionalism, high motivation, energy, and resourcefulness
- Excellent interpersonal skills with all levels of management and clients
- Demonstrated ability to work independently *and* be a team player
- Ability to work in a high-volume, fast-paced environment; to multitask; and to meet deadlines
- Excellent organizational skills

The Survey Says. . . .

I surveyed and/or interviewed over 150 business supervisors, managers, vice presidents, and presidents, asking them to describe their dream employee. They all basically said the same thing. Their expectations start with a foundation of integrity, trust, ethical behavior, and honesty. Add a positive attitude, a smile on your face, a good work ethic, and a professional appearance, and you're on your way to a successful career.

They'll expect you to meet deadlines, follow through on your commitments, pay attention to details, and do quality work. They want you to be able to think outside the box and have great organizational skills so you don't lose the box.

They'll want you to go with the flow and keep your cool when everything changes. Be confident, not cocky. Be curious, courteous, and competent. And be dedicated, dependable, and determined.

They want you to understand that excellent communication skills are a must. And being a team player is not optional. They'll want you to know it all, but not act as if you do. And this is just *part* of what employers want you to know.

PROFILE OF A DREAM EMPLOYEE

One summer, we had an open position in the community services department. We received hundreds of applications for this entry-level position and narrowed the field of candidates to four.

Monica Egert Smith had an impressive resume for a twenty-three-year-old. The other three candidates had more years of experience than Monica, but after a brief phone conversation, I knew we wanted to bring her in for an interview.

I could hardly wait to meet her in person. She walked in my office, and before she said a word, I was impressed. Her beautiful smile, professional attire, and passion for life immediately caught my attention. She had me at "hello."

We talked about her past work experience. I learned about her work ethic and how she managed challenging projects. After spending an hour with her, I knew she was the one. One of the best days of my career was when Monica accepted our offer. In the first week, I knew she was a shining star. In the first month, I knew she was the one I wanted to have my job someday.

Over the years, she became my "go to" person. She was the one I knew I could count on, no matter what. She saw everything as an opportunity, going above and beyond every single day. Monica was every manager's dream employee. She was the total package, admired and respected by everyone—internally and externally.

I can't tell you what her degree is in—all I know is she graduated from The Ohio State University. It's not what she learned in any particular class that made her special; it's what she learned about life along the way. She was the ultimate team player, earning the respect of everyone in the department. When I decided to leave the company, Monica was promoted to the leadership position. It was a dream come true for Monica, me, and the entire community services team. She had earned it.

Now it's your turn. You can be a dream employee—a star performer who has an amazing career. Do your best to be the total package. It's all up to you.

CHAPTER THREE

It's All Up to You

I f you think your bosses can't sleep at night because they are thinking about your career, think again. They aren't. They're thinking about their careers. Don't take it personally. Their bosses aren't thinking about them either.

You are responsible for your success. The *only* one who can make your dreams come true is you. What do *you* want to do? Once you decide what your career goals are, go for it. If you decide you want to be the CEO of a company, great. If you decide you don't ever want to move up the ladder, great. Success means something different to everyone. It isn't measured by your title or your salary—success is measured by the way *you* feel about *you*. Period.

Focus on what you say, not what others say. Focus on what you do, not what others do. Focus on what you have, not what they have. So many people spend countless hours thinking about what other people say, do, or have. Focus your mental energy on your dreams, goals, and passions. You have a unique blend of gifts, talents, and natural abilities. Put them to work and watch the magic unfold. It's all up to you.

WHAT DO YOU WANT TO BE KNOWN FOR?

Do you want to be known for your courage, modesty, generosity, and empathy for humankind? As someone who follows through on her commitments and always takes the high road?

Do you want to be known as a team player who has a positive, "can-do" attitude? As someone who sees everything as an opportunity and has a great work ethic? Or do you want to be known as someone who does just enough to get by, complains about everything, and never accepts responsibility for his actions because it's *never* his fault? If you owned the company, which person would you want on your team?

Do you want to be known as someone with "real worth" or "net worth"? Think about it: People who earn the most money are not necessarily the happiest people in the world. The happiest people are the ones who have *real* worth, because they make a difference in the lives of others.

Leave a legacy. We all dream of leaving a legacy, of leaving our mark on the world. You have the power to do that. Try to picture yourself twenty-five years from now. What will your story be? It all starts today.

YOUR DREAM JOB

If you've already found your dream job, congratulations! You're one of the lucky ones. Most college graduates aren't sure what they want to do in their careers. If you still don't know, it's OK. There are a lot of great career tests out there; take as many as you can. They're designed to help you identify your strengths, interests, and passions.

If you love what you're doing, it won't seem like work. What are you passionate about? What makes you want to high-five someone? What lights you up? The ultimate goal would be to find a job you love. If you're lucky, you'll find it on the first try. If your first job right out of college doesn't turn out to be your dream job, you just need some time, and possibly some direction, to figure it all out.

Picture Yourself There

When I decided to walk away from the best job in the world to start my own company, I could picture myself helping recent college graduates succeed in their lives and careers. I could picture myself having the time of my life. The vision was crystal clear, validating what my heart was telling me to do. Having the ability to picture yourself there, wherever *there* is, will help you prepare for and visualize the end result.

If you must have a tough conversation with someone, picture yourself having the actual conversation. Practice what you'll say. Think about what the other person might say, so you can think about how you'll respond.

Picture yourself ten years from now—where do you want to be? What do you want to have accomplished? If you have the ability to begin with the end in mind, you'll be able to plan carefully the steps it takes to get there.

YOU'VE GOT TO BELIEVE

You need to be your biggest fan. You need to believe in you before others will. You can do it—whatever *it* is. There's no obstacle you can't overcome. There's no challenge you can't handle.

Everything you've accomplished, everyone you've loved, every mistake you've made, every obstacle you've overcome is part of the person you are today. Be proud of who you are and what you've accomplished.

If you don't believe in you, it will impact every part of your life. Let the past be the past. Don't beat yourself up. If you make a mistake, learn from it and move on. That little voice inside your head should be saying positive, not negative things. The power is within you to be what you want to be. Hold your head high.

Over-the-Top Believing

You've got to believe, but not to the extreme. We've all been around people who act like they know everything. Would you agree they are annoying? You know a lot, but you don't know it all. No one does. Coming across as a "know-it-all" is a sure way to get labeled as arrogant or cocky. You don't want to go there. Choose a quiet confidence.

Never Give up on Your Dreams

Never let people tell you that you can't do something. How do *they* know what you can and can't do? If you want it badly enough, you can make it happen.

Spend time with people who inspire you, not those who discourage you. Don't let the noise of others' opinions drown out your inner voice. Have the courage to follow your heart and intuitions. You may come to a dead end, but don't give up. Sometimes the greatest rejections create the greatest direction. When one door closes, another opens. Your best days are ahead of you. You are full of potential and have something no one else can offer.

THE POWER OF A POSITIVE ATTITUDE

It's your attitude, not your aptitude, which will determine your success in life. In my opinion, the key to success is simple. If you have a positive attitude, see everything as an opportunity, are enthusiastic and dedicated, and work hard, you will succeed in every area of your life.

Put a positive spin on everything, and eliminate words such as "can't," "won't," and "don't." Focus on what you *can* do, what you *will* do. It's amazing what a positive attitude can do. You'll be able to see the bright side of any situation and be able to inspire and motivate yourself and others.

And you'll have the ability to handle challenges that come along in life. Notice I said "challenges," not "problems." I see them as challenges or opportunities. I rarely use the word problem, because it's such a negative word.

A positive attitude will give you more energy, and you're going to need all you can get when you start your career. Bottom line: A positive attitude leads to success and happiness.

Surround Yourself with People Who Have a Positive Attitude

Would you rather be around people who laugh and smile all the time or people who see the negative side of everything—people who are always in a bad mood and complain about everything? Which ones are more successful? The people who have a positive attitude and see the bright side.

Have you ever thought about how much mental energy people use when they're negative? No wonder they're so grouchy all the time. They focus their energy on the wrong things. Run as fast as you can from them; they will zap your mental energy. Surround yourself with successful people who have positive attitudes.

Choose to Be Happy

No one can make you happy but you. Not your best friend, your parents, your boss, or your significant other. *You* are responsible for your happiness.

The happiest people don't necessarily have the best of everything. They just make the best of what they have. Be happy where you are. Life is too short to be anything but happy. If you make up your mind to be happy, you will be. The power is within you.

LET YOUR PASSION SHINE

Whether you're in sales, working on a big project, or raising money for a great cause, if you're passionate about your work, people will *want* to be part of it. Let them see and feel your passion.

Enthusiasm is contagious. People will come out of the woodwork to participate in an atmosphere of excitement, passion, and optimism. Your success will be in direct proportion to your enthusiasm.

The Power of a Smile

Have you ever smiled at someone who didn't smile back? If so, then you probably didn't smile at them long enough. Smiles are contagious. It's almost impossible for someone not to smile back, even if they don't want to. Sometimes all it takes is a smile. That simple gesture can make someone feel special. When you get to the office, take a moment to smile and wave to the colleagues you see along the way. You have the power to make their day.

As I was driving out of the parking lot on my last day in the corporate world, the security guard stopped me. With a tear in his eye, he said, "Thank you." I smiled, and said, "Thank you for what?" He said, "Thank you for making all of us feel special. You always smile and wave when you come and go. Not many people do. We're going to miss you so much." With a tear in my eye, I got out of my car and gave him a big hug.

People love to be around people who smile. Be the person they all love to see.

Be the Breath of Fresh Air

Your passion and excitement could reignite an entire team. This is your chance to shine. One of the best things about new college graduates is that they bring innovative and creative ideas to an organization.

Be the breath of fresh air but proceed with caution. Before you start introducing your great ideas, learn the business and get to know the people. After you've earned respect and trust, if you see a better way to do something, share your ideas. Just be sure you do it in a respectful way.

Consider saying something like, "I realize we've always done X, but I think there may be a more efficient way which would save the company money." Now you have their attention. If you come up with an idea that can save time or money, they'll love you.

The Leader Within You—Let Them See It

Leaders set high standards for themselves. In every organization, there are people who are influential and respected, regardless of the title they hold. Leaders ask questions, listen carefully, have a plan, and build consensus among their colleagues. These are qualities you can have regardless of your position. Let them see the leader within you.

WORK IS NOT A FOUR-LETTER WORD

Don't get so busy you forget to have fun. You're going to spend a lot of time at work, so make the most of it. Take your job seriously, but have fun while you're doing it. The one thing that I know I'm going to do every single day of my life is have fun.

Think about your best days. You know, the days where you are on top of the world and loving life. What happened? My best days are when I'm making a presentation and I have an impact on the audience. Or the days when a recent college graduate calls or e-mails to tell me that something I said changed his or her life. Those are my best days. What are yours? When you have one of your best days, figure out what happened, and do more of it. Try to make every day a great day.

Take good care of yourself. It will help you avoid burnout. Cherish your friends, love your family, and enjoy your hobbies. Your career is one part of your life, but it's not the only way to define your success. Life is short, so enjoy the journey. Cherish every precious moment.

Laughter Is Good for the Soul

You need to laugh—a lot. Laughter connects us with others and is contagious. It can cause a domino effect of joy and excitement, and a good laugh reduces stress and provides instant relaxation. There are even medical benefits of laughter, including lowering your blood pressure, boosting your immune system, and improving your brain functions. Bottom line: Laughter makes people feel good.

Don't take life too seriously. You're going to do some embarrassing things along the way, and you have to be able to laugh at yourself.

I learned to laugh at myself early in my career. I was twenty-two and working for Dallas Power & Light. The company was involved in the United Way, and I volunteered to raise money for the campaign. I was attending an orientation session, and the speaker kept using an acronym I didn't understand. After she used it the third time, I raised my hand. "Excuse me, what does CEO stand for?"

All the heads in the room (all two hundred of them) turned to see who asked the question. The speaker then answered, "It stands for chief executive officer."

In that moment, I knew why all those eyes were on me. I had just asked a *really* dumb question. Perhaps I should have known what CEO stood for, but it wasn't a term I was taught in college, and it wasn't something I'd heard in my short nine months on the job. I was mortified then, but it was easy to laugh about it later. You, too, will have embarrassing moments. Get over them. They're not the end of the world.

Just Because You Think It's Funny Doesn't Mean Others Will

I love to make people laugh and smile. Humor definitely has a place in the work world, as long as it's used appropriately. Have you ever heard someone tell a funny story, but at the same time, it embarrassed someone? Perhaps that someone was you. You probably didn't like the way it made you feel.

I have a good friend who always has to be the "funny guy." There are times when he is funny, but often the laughter embarrasses someone. When this happens, it's awkward for everyone. People are laughing only because they don't know what else to do.

Don't make fun of people. It's embarrassing—for you and the other person. Remember to laugh *with* people, not at them. There's a big difference between the two.

WANTING IT ALL—NOW!

You want a great job with all the good stuff: career growth opportunities, vacation time, a nice salary, great medical benefits, and a retirement plan. You want to work on interesting, challenging projects in a comfortable environment and have a management team that is accessible. A flexible work schedule would be great, too. And how about a promotion in the first six months on the job? Good luck.

You may get all this in your first job, but you may not. Be patient. You're anxious to succeed in your career, and your ambitious goals are a good thing, but you'll be more successful in a leadership position if you slowly work your way up to the top.

Why You Don't Want to Be the CEO in the First Five Years:

- How can you expect to lead an entire organization successfully when you haven't been there long enough to know how all the parts work?

- The expectations and demands are enormous. Do you *really* want to work 24/7?

- Successful CEOs have relationships with people throughout the entire organization. Have you been there long enough to develop those relationships? You need time to earn trust and respect.

- If you're the CEO when you're twenty-seven, what will you do when you're thirty-five?

- It can be lonely at the top.

When I was a freshman in college, I took an advanced-placement math class. I made an A, which meant I received nine hours of credit and placed out of two math classes. I thought it was great, until I took calculus my sophomore year. One of the classes I placed out of was trigonometry. Those of you who took calculus know you have to be good at trig in order to understand *anything* about calculus. I suffered through two semesters of calculus because of my decision to advance too quickly.

As you look at your career, I encourage you to take your time and experience every "class" offered to you. I know you may be anxious to move up the ladder, but if you skip the middle part, you'll suffer when you're at the top. You must earn your seat at the big table. You wouldn't want it any other way.

CHAPTER FOUR

THE CORE COUNTS

—— ◆ ——

Your reputation is a shadow that follows you through life—always remember that. You want to earn a reputation as someone of honesty, integrity, respect, and trust. When you put these qualities together, they make a nice package. It's the package every employer is looking for. Make sure it's the package you have to offer.

The most important investment you'll make in life is in your integrity. It's what leads people to trust you and be willing to rely on you. Without personal and professional integrity, you won't go very far in life. The most important thing about integrity is that once you've lost it, it's *very* hard to get back.

What exactly is integrity? In the business world, integrity is defined more by actions than by anything else. You can show you have it by these actions:

- Following through on your commitments
- Taking responsibility for your mistakes

- Giving credit to others

- Doing consistently high-quality work

- Knowing when to listen and when to speak

- Not letting your boss or co-workers down

- Being honest and ethical

You'll make a million decisions over the course of your career. On your journey, be sure to use good judgment. Use your common sense. Stop and think before you do anything that would put your reputation at risk.

You can be whatever you want to be—just be sure you do it with humility, honesty, integrity, respect, and kindness.

Prove It

You know you can do the job. Why can't they see it? They hired you because you were the best candidate for the job. But remember, they hired you based on what they learned about you in a one-hour interview. Now they want to see you in action. They believe you can do it, but they won't know for sure until you prove yourself.

Your parents didn't hand you the keys to the car without some practice driving time. You had to prove you knew the rules of the road. The same is true in your career. Respect and trust are not things that automatically come with your degree. They have to be earned.

Prove yourself everyday. Not just for them; do it for you.

It's Just a Box of Paperclips

So what's the big deal? It's just a box of paperclips. Seriously, how much does it cost the company? It's not the cost that's important, it's the principle. If someone sees you taking a box of paperclips home, they may wonder what else you've taken. Or what else you might plan to take. It's not worth it.

Before you even think about doing something that would put your reputation at risk, think about the box of paperclips.

THE HIDDEN CAMERA

What if every move you made was being taped for the whole world to see—your boss, your colleagues, your friends, and your family? If that were the case, would you do some of the things you do? Would you say some of the things you say?

What if every call you made was recorded to assure quality customer service? What if every e-mail you sent was seen by the CEO of your organization? What if the person you decided to torment on the highway because he cut you off turned out to be the potential client you had to meet with this afternoon? What if your client wasn't actually on hold when you made a negative comment about her?

Be careful what you say; be careful what you do. You never know who might be watching. When you're out in public, you never know who's at the next table.

What if the person at the next table is the best friend of the person you're whining about? What if the person at the next table is the secretary of the guy you just interviewed with for a new job? What if you're up for a promotion and someone overheard you trashing your boss? You just never know whom they know, so be careful.

Remember when you were a little kid and you did something wrong? You thought there was no way your parents would find out, but they did. The same holds true for your employer.

What if everything you said, everything you did, was a test? A test to see if you were ready for the next step—a raise, a promotion, or a new job opportunity. You never know when someone else is watching. Live your life as if everything were being seen on a hidden camera. If you start thinking that way, it's amazing the things you won't do or say.

Here's another way to look at it. Live your life as if someday you plan to run for political office. You may be thinking, "There is *no* way I'll ever run for office." But what if you marry someone who decides to run for office? They'll look into your background as well as your spouse's.

Never say anything about someone you wouldn't say if they were sitting next to you. You want to be known for your integrity. The decisions you make today will be with you for the rest of your life.

ALWAYS TAKE THE HIGH ROAD

Taking the high road means you do the right thing, say the right thing, and treat others with respect at all times. And it means you don't say *anything* bad about anyone. If you slip just one time and say something negative about someone, it could leave people wondering what you say about them behind their backs.

One night, I experienced the true high-road test. My son was a senior in high school, and I was at his football game. In addition to being a linebacker, he was also the long snapper. Chris was having a great game on defense, but his first long snap sailed over the punter's head. Three guys sitting behind me started ragging on Chris. They were shouting, "Oh, come on! That was horrible. Can't you do any better than that?" My blood started to boil.

Several plays later, Chris went back on the field for another punt. Before Chris ever got his hands on the ball, these guys start shouting, "Are there any long snappers in the stands? Number 95 obviously can't do it." My blood was *really* boiling now. This long snap was a good one.

I have a tremendous amount of patience, but if someone starts messing with my kids, it dwindles—almost immediately. I sat there, getting madder and madder. Then, I said to myself, "Be careful, Nancy. You represent *The Dallas Morning News* and WFAA twenty-four hours a day, seven days a week. Don't say anything stupid."

I don't even want to tell you what I wanted to say to these guys. They had probably never played a down of football in their lives but thought they knew more than the players or coaches. During half time, I cooled down a bit and regained my composure. When I sat down, I turned around and tapped one of the guys on the knee. He looked my way. I smiled and said, "Excuse me, could you take it easy on Number 95? He's my son." As I was explaining the family connection, I was also showing him the button on my jacket with Chris's picture on it.

You should have seen the look on his face. He stuttered a bit and said, "Oh, oh, it was just that *one* play; he's really had a great game."

Shortly after our conversation, Chris intercepted the ball and ran for a touchdown. These guys went crazy and leaned over to give me a high-five. All of a sudden, they acted as if they were part of our family. Over the years, I've seen these guys out in the neighborhood, and they enthusiastically ask, "How's Chris doing?"

That night, I learned that no matter what happens, you need to stay on the high road. There's no telling how many lessons those guys learned.

Another day, one of my colleagues had the ultimate high-road test. It was during a time when we were in fierce competition with another newspaper in the market. She had been to a meeting where representatives from our competitor spoke poorly of our company.

She left me a voice mail saying, "Nancy, I need you to call me as soon as you can. I *know* we're supposed to stay on the high road, but I have one toe in the gravel." There will be days when you may veer off the high road. Steer back on as fast as you can. You'll be glad you did.

WHAT *WERE* THEY THINKING?

We've all seen stories in the media about people who have lied. You can't help but think, "What *were* they thinking?"

Take, for example, the guy who ran a Fortune 500 company. It turned out he didn't graduate with the degree listed on his resume. And we're talking about the *president* of the company—now the *former* president of the company.

Or the female executive who took advantage of a stock tip, was prosecuted, and ended up serving time in prison. Or the elected official who sent an inappropriate e-mail, thinking he was having a private exchange. He denied the entire incident, until the private little e-mail was shared on the national news for everyone to see.

What *were* they thinking? They weren't. You will.

Tell the Truth, Even if It's Scary

Another key to living on the high road is to tell the truth, the whole truth and nothing but the truth. Think about the people who have lied to you over the years. How many lies did it take before they lost your trust? How many lies did it take before it was hard to believe anything they had to say?

I've known people who would tell a lie even if the truth sounded better. Once you start telling *little* lies, it leads to telling *big* lies. There will be times when you'll want to lie. You're scared. You may think your career is on the line. But if you always tell the truth, no matter how painful it might seem at the moment, you'll be glad you did.

There was an employee who called in, about once a week, with excuses as to why she'd be late to work. The manager suspected her excuses were lies, but had no proof. Until one day, the employee called to let her manager know she had a doctor's appointment and would be in the office around 10 a.m. At noon, the employee called to say she'd been waiting for three hours to see the doctor. She forgot that the manager had Caller ID on his phone, and he could tell she was calling from home. (Ouch.)

YOU MADE A MISTAKE—NOW WHAT?

We all make mistakes. That's how we learn. When you make one, learn from it, and move on. It's important to remember you are human. You're going to make mistakes, and the people you work with are going to make them, too. The key is accepting responsibility for your actions. There are a lot of people out there who play "the blame game." It's *always* someone else's fault.

Many years ago, one of my bosses taught me a valuable lesson. He said, "Nancy, if you ever make a mistake and tick someone off, just say these words: 'I take complete responsibility.' If you say those words, it completely disarms the other person. There's really nothing else for them to say."

Those words of wisdom came in handy one day when I made one of my big, big bosses mad. *Really, really mad.* I made a decision he didn't agree with. We were on the phone, and he was doing all the talking (yelling). I didn't say a word. When he finally stopped yelling, I said, "I take complete responsibility." That was the end of the conversation. He hesitated, then said, "OK," and hung up.

To this day, I believe the decision I made was a good one, but it didn't matter. He was my boss, and it was my responsibility to do what *he* thought was best. Period.

In addition to taking responsibility for your actions, you could add something like, "In retrospect, I should have handled this differently. I've learned a valuable lesson, and it won't happen again."

If you make a mistake, people expect you to have an excuse or try to blame it on someone else. Surprise them—take complete responsibility. At that moment, you have earned the respect of the other person.

Don't Be So Hard on Yourself

You're not perfect; you're human. If something goes wrong, don't beat yourself up. Learn from it. Apologize, if appropriate. Do what's right and move on.

Things will happen that will seem like a big deal at the time. You'll spend days worrying about it, and weeks later you won't even remember what happened. Trust me, it'll blow over. You'll forget about it, and so will your boss. (Unless you've done something really bad, and then you'll need more than this book to help you!)

When you make a mistake, don't be so hard on yourself. Always ask yourself, "Is the world going to come to an end if _____?" No matter what you put in the blank, the answer will always be "no."

Ask yourself, "Is this really such a big deal?" You'll be harder on yourself than anyone else will ever be on you. It's like when you finish a big project, and then you find the one little thing that went wrong. And it's all you can think about. Stop it. Turn off the negative voice in your head.

Don't focus on what went wrong, focus on what went right. Write down all the things you've done right over the last month. Then write down what you've done wrong. Which list is longer? I feel sure the list of things you've done right is longer. Give yourself some credit. Celebrate your successes. Try not to focus on the wrong stuff.

On the other hand, if the list of things you've done wrong is fairly long, take some time to analyze what's going on. Do you see any patterns? What are the areas in which you could improve? We all need improvement.

Take your career seriously, and do the very best you can, but don't be so hard on yourself. Learn from mistakes and move on.

ZERO TOLERANCE

There are certain things in life which should not and will not be tolerated. Your employer may give you an employee handbook listing areas of zero tolerance. Just in case they don't have a policy, here's my list:

- Offensive remarks

- Being disrespectful

- Discrimination of any kind

- Theft

- Profanity

- Falsifying documents

- Sharing confidential information

Enough said.

YOU WANT ME TO DO WHAT?!

Along the way, you will be asked to do something, and you may think, "You want me to do what?!" A lot of college graduates are under the impression that after they walk across the stage and get their diplomas, they are entitled to no longer have to get their hands dirty. They act as if they are too good to do certain things.

This may be the most important advice in this book: Never, ever think you are too good to do anything. Be the one who always has a positive attitude, no matter what needs to be done. There are a lot of employers who expect you to have an "entitlement attitude." Surprise them by not having one. Your strong work ethic will separate you from the rest of the pack.

I have a friend who owns her own public relations firm, and she has told me she'll no longer hire recent college graduates because of their attitudes. Once she was planning a big event, and just before it started, she asked her new employee to sweep up some stuff on the floor. The employee looked at her and asked, "Aren't there *other* people to do that?"

If someone needs copies made for a presentation, just smile and say, "I'd be more than happy to make them. How many copies do you need? When would you like to have them?" At the time, you may be thinking, "I did *not* go to college to make copies." But your body language needs to be saying, "I'd be happy to make the copies." If your ultimate goal is to own your own business, you'll be the one doing all this stuff anyway. Consider it an investment in your future.

I'll tell you why you should *want* to be the one to make the copies.

- You'll develop a reputation for having a "can-do" attitude. Managers love that. You'll be the one that ends up getting all the dream projects, because your managers and colleagues know they can count on you.

- You may be the only one smart enough to work the new copy machine. Think of it as job security.

- You'll have the opportunity to participate in a brainless activity. It'll give you a chance to get out of your office and be in a new environment—the copy center.

- And there's no telling whom you might meet in the copy room.

See everything as an opportunity. Be willing to get your hands dirty.

BECOME A "GO TO" PERSON

If you want to stand out above the crowd, and be loved by every manager you work with, become what I call a "go to" person. That's someone who is known for having a positive attitude, meeting deadlines, and always following through on commitments they've made. The more you do, the more you'll *get* to do. You'll also get exposure at a level in the company you may not have had before.

About three months after I joined *The Dallas Morning News*, the publisher asked me to work on a special project. Needless to say, I was thrilled to have the opportunity to work with him. He was pleased with the work I did, and I quickly became his "go to" person. We worked on some wonderful projects together, including planning a national convention for publishers from across the country.

I was fortunate to develop a relationship with the publisher early in my career. As a result, I was promoted to vice president of community services after only three years with the company. Never pass up the opportunity to work on new projects. No matter how busy you are, make the time to do it. It's a fabulous opportunity to prove yourself. If you become known as a "go to" person early in your career, all kinds of magical things could happen.

A dear friend, who owns his own business, learned a valuable lesson from his dad. "Never give people a reason to call someone else." It's great advice for all of us.

WELCOME FEEDBACK

We all say we want feedback, but when someone gives it to us, we're not so sure we really want it. Your first instinct may be to defend yourself, fight back, or give the person critiquing you the silent treatment. We have a tendency to hear only the bad stuff. Listen for the good things.

Deep down inside, we all want to be perfect, but that's not a healthy goal. No one is perfect. There's always room for improvement. You can learn and grow from others' experiences and perspectives. As tough as it can be to hear criticism, it's essential in every relationship, especially in the workplace. Since nobody's perfect, everybody needs to know what he or she could do better. Feedback can be a powerful tool for enhancing your job performance, providing personal and professional development.

I've seen people over the years who get defensive when someone gives them feedback, no matter how gently the suggestions are made. I've seen them cut people off in the middle of a sentence to protect themselves. It's a natural defense mechanism, so the person won't question something you have or haven't done. But if someone is trying to give you feedback, resist the urge to immediately defend yourself. Listen to what they're saying.

If you continue to reject feedback, people won't want to work with you. Some managers will take the time to coach you, but a lot of managers won't. They'll just start slowly pulling away, and you'll become a "work around." They won't have the time or the energy to deal with you, so they'll stop giving you assignments. They'll decide it's just not worth it—the drama, the whining, the missed deadlines, and the excuses.

So when someone offers feedback, listen up. It may not feel good at the moment. But take some time to let it sink in, and I guarantee you, there will be a nugget of gold somewhere in there.

CHAPTER FIVE

LIKE IT OR NOT, THIS STUFF MATTERS

Like it or not, people are constantly judging us. They make judgments based on whether we arrive on time to a meeting. They judge us by our handshakes. They judge us by the way we look—our clothes, our hair, and our jewelry. They make decisions about us based on whether we look them in the eye when we're speaking, and by the tone in our voices. We may not like it, but this stuff matters.

Your professional image influences the way others respond to you. You want to project an image that will impress your clients, your employer, and your co-workers. Don't just do it for them, do it for you. Looking your best helps you feel positive about who you are as a person. When you look and feel your best, it's amazing what you can accomplish.

FIRST IMPRESSIONS—YOU GET ONE CHANCE

We've all heard about the importance of first impressions. You have *one* chance to get it right. Business experts say you have seven seconds to make a good first impression. What happens in those seven seconds?

The first thing people notice is whether you arrive on time. Then they notice other details: Are you smiling? Are you looking them in the eye? Do you have a good handshake? And before you ever say a word, your appearance is speaking for you. Your first impression lasts a long time, so make the most of it. You never have a second chance to make a good first impression.

Your Handshake Matters

A good handshake makes a difference. When you offer someone a firm, palm-to-palm handshake, coupled with eye contact and a smile, you appear to be confident, interested, and sincere. Throughout my career, I've had the opportunity to meet a lot of people. I am always amazed at the number of people—young and old—who don't know how to properly shake hands.

There are all kinds of handshakes out there. There's the limp handshake, the pincher, and the bone-crusher. I never know what to do when someone gives me a limp handshake. I'm not sure if I should hold on or just let go. And the pinchers drive me crazy. I *want* to give someone a good handshake, but I can't because they pinched the tips of my fingers before I could ever get in there to shake their hand.

And over the years, there have been times I've almost had tears in my eyes when some big guy, who is ten times stronger than I am, shakes my hand and almost crushes it.

If you're in a meeting and you just crushed the hand of your manager or co-worker, she won't care what a great job you did on the project. All she'll be thinking about is how much pain she is in.

The Key to a Handshake That Will Make a Good Impression

Look the person in the eye, smile, and shake hands. (You shouldn't have to look at your hand connecting with the other person's.) Open your hand enough to be able to connect fully with the other person's. Once you're in there, firmly close your fingers around the hand and pump one time. You don't have to go on and on with the pumping part.

This may sound crazy, but if you have a good handshake, you'll be ahead of most people in the world.

DRESS-CODE DILEMMA

Why should it matter what you wear? Didn't they hire you because of who you are and what you can offer their company, rather than the clothes you have on? Maybe it shouldn't matter so much, but it does. You want people to focus on you, not your clothes, shoes, fingernails, jewelry, tattoos, or body piercings.

The first thing people see is your smile and the sparkle in your eyes. The second thing they see is your clothes. If you aren't dressed professionally, you may appear not to take them seriously. You *want* your boss, clients, and colleagues to take you seriously.

Was your interview the last time you wore your best clothes? That's not good! They hired you based on what they saw during your interview. You need to continue to be that person. You want the management of your organization to know from the start that you are serious about who you are and what you want to accomplish.

If you owned your own company, would you want to do business with someone who didn't care about appearance? Your first response might be, "It wouldn't matter to me." But if you think about it, it does matter.

Figuring Out the Dress Code

How do they expect you to know what to wear when they never gave you the guidelines? What does "business casual" mean? If you can't figure out the dress code, you're going to be at an immediate disadvantage.

Look around. What's your manager wearing? Don't base your decision on what your co-workers are wearing. For all you know, they may be on probation for not wearing the proper attire. Every organization has a different dress code, so be sure you know what's appropriate for *this* job. If you are in doubt, ask your manager what's appropriate. She will love you for asking before she has to say something about your attire.

I've never met anyone who was criticized for looking professional. I have, however, met people who lost their jobs because they refused to comply with the guidelines. Your attire says a lot about how much you respect yourself, your company, and your clients. What if your attire turned off a client and you lost the sale and your commissions? It matters. If you want to move to the next level someday, dress the part now.

It's a little dangerous to dress for what you *think* is going to happen on any given day. Let's say you decided to come to work dressed casually, because you didn't have any meetings with clients. What if something different happens? What if the client you've been courting for the last six months calls at the last minute and wants to meet with you? What if the chairman of your organization (whom you've never met) calls and wants you to come to her office? It could happen.

General Guidelines on Attire

The main thing to remember is that you don't ever want to wear anything distracting. That includes clothes that are wrinkled, too tight, or too flashy. Avoid clothes that are skimpy or revealing. You want your colleagues and clients to focus on you and your talents, not on your body.

Make sure your shirt covers the top of your pants, so your midsection doesn't show. Your shirt may cover you up when you're standing, but what happens when you sit down? Do the "sit-down test." It works for shirts and skirts. If the test shows your outfit is a distraction, choose something else to wear.

When in doubt, go the conservative route. You'll never get in trouble for dressing too conservatively, but you could be put in an embarrassing situation if you dress too casually. It's always better to be a bit overdressed than underdressed. Have a jacket with you. You can always take it off if you don't need it, but if you find you need one and didn't bring it, you are out of luck.

Before you leave home, look in a full-length mirror and ask yourself, "If I'm called to the president's office today, will she be comfortable with what I'm wearing?" Notice I didn't say, "Will *you* be comfortable?" I said, "Will *she* be comfortable?"

As you're standing in front of that full-length mirror, take a moment to see how you look from the back. Make sure you don't have any visible panty/boxer lines that would be distracting as you walk down the hall at work. I'm convinced a lot of people don't take that second look in the mirror. You know what I'm talking about.

Work Clothes Versus Weekend Clothes

After you have a clear understanding of what you should wear to work, take time to organize your closet. Put your work clothes on one side and your weekend clothes on the other. That way you won't be tempted to wear the wrong thing.

OTHER STUFF THAT MATTERS

Your Hair

When I first started my career, I had long blonde hair. An older woman (40 years older) took me aside and told me I needed to cut my hair because it didn't look professional. At first, I was angry. Who was *she* to tell me what I should do with my hair? But after I had a chance to cool off and think about it, I realized she was right. My hair was great for my college days, but wasn't necessarily a look that would cause people in the workplace to take me seriously.

If you want your colleagues and clients to take you seriously, take a look at your hair. Be sure the style is not distracting. The same holds true for your hair color. If you choose to color your hair, make sure it looks natural.

For the guys, I know your college days may have been the last time you could have long hair. I also know how painful it was when you had to cut it for upcoming interviews. Things like this make you want to call your college years "the glory days." But like it or not, your hairstyle does matter.

Your Shoes, Fragrance, Makeup, and Fingernails

You want them to focus on you, not the fact that your shoes are not in good shape. You want them to focus on you, not the overwhelming scent of your fragrance.

Ladies, remember there's a difference between daytime and evening makeup. During the workday, don't wear too much. You want people to notice you, not your makeup.

Keep in mind that we use our hands all day. We talk with our hands, we place our hands on the top of the conference room table during meetings, and we use our hands to enjoy a business meal. You want to make sure your nails are neatly groomed, so they aren't a distraction.

Body Piercings

The piercings you have on various parts of your body are your business. But just know, if you have a piercing anywhere on your face, I'm not going to hear anything you say. All I'm going to be thinking is, "Gosh that must hurt!" Enough said.

Tattoos

A friend of mine was interviewing a job candidate. It was a great interview, until the very end. When the candidate got ready to leave, she bent down to pick up her purse and accidentally revealed her large, lower-back tattoo.

All of a sudden, *nothing* the candidate had said mattered. All my friend could remember was the tattoo and the fact that the clothing the candidate chose to wear didn't cover her body. Perhaps it shouldn't matter, but it does.

If somewhere along the way you decided to get a tattoo, keep it covered at work. It's distracting.

BUSINESS MANNERS MATTER

Your professional image will also be measured by your business etiquette skills. There are many wonderful books out there about business etiquette. You can find a list of some of my favorites on my Web site, www.nancybarry.com.

I'll give you the highlights.

Be on Time

Being on time is one of the most important things you'll do in life. When planning traveling time, factor in school zones, traffic delays, flat tires, and so on. If you're going to be late, call. If you are constantly late, it's going to catch up to you one day.

If your manager asks you to be at work by 8 a.m., that means she wants you to be at your desk at 8 a.m., not pulling into the parking lot. If you have a tendency to be late, tell yourself you have to be at work at 7:45 a.m. Then if you're running late, you may actually be on time.

And always arrive on time for meetings. Arriving late is disrespectful to everyone involved. If you are constantly late to meetings, you may find your manager starts locking the door.

Respond to Invitations

I'm shocked by the number of people—young and old—who never take the time to RSVP. If someone is kind enough to invite you to an event, you should be kind enough to let them know whether or not you're coming.

If you were planning a party and no one called to let you know if they'd be able to attend, how would you be able to make plans for the party? Be courteous and take the time to reply.

Electronic Device Etiquette

Your cell phone is your lifeline. You feel lost without it. You're addicted to your BlackBerry. Brace yourself: I'm about to tell you some things you *don't* want to hear.

We've all seen them—people who think they have to have their cell phones, BlackBerries, pagers, and any other new electronic device on at all times. Are they really *that* important? Put your phone on vibrate or silent when you're at the office. Or here's a radical idea: Consider turning if off. Refrain from taking calls when you're in a meeting. The people you are with should be your total focus. If you take a call, the people you're with are not going to feel valued. If you're expecting a call that can't be postponed, let people know in advance.

Have a professional ring tone, just in case you forget to put your phone on silent. If your ring tone is wild and your phone rings in the middle of your vice president's presentation, you're going to be embarrassed. And avoid walking down the hallways at work talking about the date you had last night.

Monitor the volume of your voice. Why do people shout when they're on a cell phone? I'm guilty of this. It drives my kids crazy. I must consciously remember to tone down when I'm on my cell phone. If you're in a public place, remember everyone around you can hear your conversation, so be careful. Also, if you're out in public using one of those hands-free devices, you look like you're crazy. When you ask, "How are you today?" don't be surprised if the person walking down the street next to you responds.

If you're in the car with a co-worker or client, don't talk on your cell phone the whole time. This is your chance to have a conversation. Many years ago, my big boss asked me to go to a meeting with him. Since he wasn't my direct boss, I didn't get a chance to spend much one-on-one time with him. I was so excited that I was going to have a chance to visit with him. As soon as we got in the car though, he started returning phone calls. He talked on his phone the *entire* time we were in the car. At that moment, I told myself I would never do that to someone. No matter who it was.

And one more thing—please don't use your BlackBerry while you're in a meeting. It's rude. The same applies to sending text messages on your cell phone. Put yourself in the shoes of the person making the presentation. You wouldn't want to see people looking down and typing with their thumbs.

IS THAT YOUR NAPKIN OR MINE?

A business dinner may appear to be social time, but the people you're with will be evaluating your every move. Whether you're on a job interview or dining with a client, your social skills, conversation, and manners will be evaluated. Business manners matter. Your table manners could make or break a job offer or a big deal being discussed.

The Table Setting

You want to be sure you know which utensils, plates, and glasses are yours. Don't be embarrassed if you don't already know this stuff. Over the years, I've attended thousands of events, and there have been many times when a high-level executive has leaned over and whispered in my ear, "Nancy, is that your napkin or mine?" They don't know, either.

When you sit down at the table, everything directly in front of you belongs to you. Your challenge will be to determine which bread plate is yours, which water glass is yours, and which coffee cup is holding your napkin. With your hands in your lap, make a circle with each thumb and index finger. The other three fingers on each hand will follow along by standing straight up. You'll notice your right hand is making a "d" and your left hand is making a "b." Your <u>D</u>rinks will be on your right and your <u>B</u>read plate will be on your left.

Is that your napkin or mine? Your napkin will either be folded under the silverware on the left, lying on the plate in front of you, or folded like a bird in your coffee cup—which you now know is on your right.

Other Things That Matter

Utensils

- Start with the utensils on the outside and work your way in.

- Your dessert fork and/or spoon is generally placed at the top of your place setting.

- Once everyone at your table has been served and your host picks up her fork, you can begin eating.

- Never place a used utensil on the table; place it on your plate.

- When you're finished with your meal, place your fork and knife together in the center of the plate. This signals to the wait staff that you are finished.

Your Napkin

- Upon sitting down, put your napkin in your lap with the fold near your waist. If you're at a formal affair, wait until the host puts his napkin in his lap.

- If you end up without a napkin because someone took yours, quietly ask one of the guests to pass you the napkin which ended up on the other side of the table. Don't make a big deal out of it, or someone will be embarrassed.

- If you get up during dinner, put your napkin on your chair. When you finish the meal, place your napkin to the left of your plate.

A Few More Tips

- Food should be passed to the right. But if someone starts going the wrong way, just go with the flow.

- The salt and pepper are a couple—they are passed together.

- Cut only the portion of food you plan to eat at the moment.

- Break your bread into three or four pieces before buttering it. When the butter is passed, take what you need and put it on your bread or salad plate. The little fork that's passed with the butter stays with the butter.

Those Rolls Could Get You in Trouble

One of my friends was interviewing a job candidate over lunch. She asked him to pass her a roll. Instead of passing her the basket, he picked up a roll and put it on her plate. In that moment, she decided that he was not getting the job. Business manners matter.

A Few Tips about Cocktail Receptions

Eat a little something before you go. If you're living on love and loans, you may see this as an opportunity for free food. But the main purpose for attending the event is not to eat; it's to build and nurture relationships. Trying to meet new people while juggling a plate of food and a drink and leaving a hand free to shake is going to be extremely hard.

It's OK to eat; just don't load up your little plate as if it's your last meal. If you're at an event where hors d'oeuvres are passed, only tackle the ones you know you can eat without embarrassing yourself. I learned this the hard way.

I was attending a cocktail reception and made a poor decision to try to gracefully eat a cherry tomato. As I bit down on the tomato, the juice projected two feet out of my mouth onto the jacket of the woman I was talking to. I was so embarrassed. Fortunately, she was a close friend, and we both laughed. But every time I see a cherry tomato, I think about her beautiful jacket. Just remember, certain foods are meant to be eaten in the privacy of your own home.

CHAPTER SIX

AVOIDING A COMMUNICATION CRISIS

◆

Excellent communication skills are some of the most valued assets in the workplace and are critical to your success. You might be the smartest person in the room, but if you can't communicate, you'll be at a disadvantage. No matter what position you hold, you're going to spend the rest of your life communicating. Your ability to speak, write, and listen on a professional level will help you gain greater recognition and give you the power you need to succeed.

When you're communicating, it's important you don't lose the personal touch. So much is now communicated through e-mails, instant messages, and text messages, but *nothing* takes the place of personal contact. There's a lot of important nonverbal communication that can take place only when you're face-to-face or on the phone.

People say a lot through their facial expressions, body language, or tone of voice. Still, there will be times when you need or want to communicate electronically. When you do, be careful of the tone of the message, which comes through in writing as well as in face-to-face interaction.

Communication is at the heart of everything we do. Make good communication skills a priority. They can make or break your career.

COMMUNICATION IS NOT "ONE SIZE FITS ALL"

Some people want to engage in small talk, and some people want to get down to business. Some people want to speak once a day, and some people want to speak once a week. Some people like e-mail, and some people can't stand it. Some people like sound bites of information, and some people want all the details. The key thing to remember is that it's all about the people you work with. You need to communicate with them in the way *they* prefer.

It's your job to find out what their preferred communication method is. You can either ask them directly, or you can observe the way they communicate. For example, if they left you a voice mail, respond via voice mail. If they sent you an e-mail, respond via e-mail. If someone left you a voice mail and you reply via e-mail, they may not get the message right away. Until you know otherwise, you need to assume they've communicated with you in their preferred style.

When I was with *The Dallas Morning News* and WFAA-TV, I had lots of bosses. And they *all* had different communication styles. One of my bosses liked bullet-point overviews but wanted you to have all the details just in case he needed them later. One of my bosses loved to have quick updates in person. Another one wanted detailed reports with little face-to-face time.

Communication can be challenging, but it's *our* job to adjust to *their* style.

Multi-Generational Communication

There are four generations in today's workforce. What's appropriate for a twenty-four-year-old in marketing might not be the same for the sixty-year-old in accounting. Each generation has its preferred style. Just be as professional as possible, in all forms of communication.

If your communication style is different from that of the people at your company, you need to be the one to adjust. I know it's not what you want to hear, but it's true if you want to be successful in your career.

Having the Ability to Communicate at All Levels Will Be a Tremendous Asset

One of the keys to your success will be your ability to form relationships with everyone, regardless of the positions they hold. You need to have the ability to communicate with all levels in the organization.

If having a conversation with the CEO makes you a little nervous, you're normal. A lot of people are intimidated by the top leadership. Don't be. They are human beings, just like the folks who turn the lights out at the end of the day.

WORKPLACE WRITING 101

While in college, you undoubtedly wrote some great papers, but the writing style in the workplace is different. You've also spent a lot of time text messaging, writing in abbreviations. It's a habit you'll need to break.

You'll need to master writing memos, reports, letters, etc. Unless you took a business communication class in college, chances are you haven't had any experience with this type of communication. Even if you did take a business writing class, you won't know everything you need to know until you've had some experience in the work world.

Do *whatever* it takes to be sure your written communication is professional. Ask your manager for samples you can follow. Pay attention to what your manager sends out. Get a good book on business communication. Attend a business writing seminar.

You'll need to write with clarity and conciseness, while using the appropriate style and tone. Grammar and punctuation are key. Proofread your work. If you're preparing an important document, ask one of your colleagues to proofread it, too. Two sets of eyes are better than one. Your ability to communicate in writing on a professional level is critical to your success.

Please note: Tone and style in business writing vary depending on your audience. For instance, this book uses a conversational, casual tone—with informalities such as sentence fragments—that wouldn't be appropriate for written communication with your clients, boss, or colleagues. If you're ever in doubt, choose a formal, stringently grammatical style until you've had several back-and-forth e-mails or letters. Then you can start adapting to and mirroring your audience.

E-MAILS—ELEVEN THINGS YOU NEED TO KNOW

1. *An E-mail Should Be as Professional as a Letter.*

Your e-mail should be simple and to the point. Put the most important information in the first paragraph. Take the time to check grammar and spelling. It'll take about ten seconds and could save you some embarrassing moments. Keep in mind, e-mails written in all lower case are too casual, and if you use all upper case, it'll seem as though you're screaming.

2. *E-mails Are Not Private Conversations.*

Never, ever put anything in an e-mail you wouldn't want the CEO to see. Never say or write anything you wouldn't want the whole world to know. And never include confidential information in an e-mail. It can be easily forwarded and could end up in the hands of the wrong person.

We've all heard horror stories about people who sent e-mails that ended up in the wrong hands. Don't let it happen to you. They are *so* easy to forward. The person on the other end might not take the time to think about whether there's any inappropriate information in your original e-mail. Yours could end up in a long e-mail trail, possibly a trail you won't want to travel.

3. *The Subject Line Is Important.*

The subject line should be a brief summary of what's in the e-mail. Rather than "Good morning" use "Client report you requested."

If there's a long e-mail trail and the subject changes midstream, update the subject line. It'll make it easier to find the e-mail you're looking for later. For people who receive hundreds of e-mails a day, the subject line may be the only way they'll find your e-mail again.

4. *Limit Copies and Blind Copies.*

One thing that drives people crazy in the workplace is the inappropriate use of the copy (cc) and blind copy (bcc) lines. Here are some general guidelines to follow. The people directly involved in the information you're sending should be listed in the "To" line. People who have specifically asked to be copied, or people who you think *need* to know the contents of the e-mail, should be listed in the "Copy" line. One of the reasons e-mails are out of control is the unnecessary copies. Use your best judgment.

The "Blind Copy" line seems sneaky to me. The only time you should use the blind copy line is if you're sending out a mass e-mail and want to protect the addresses of the recipients.

These words of wisdom come from a close friend: When sending an e-mail to your boss, never blind copy your boss's boss. She had an employee who blind copied the CEO on an e-mail outlining a proposal for a charity event my friend had already decided not to support. When the CEO hit the "reply all" button with his opinion, it revealed the employee's name. This was not the first time it had happened, but it was the first time there was proof. Within a few months, the employee was no longer with the company.

5. *E-mails Can Take Over Your Life.*

Check your e-mail regularly, but don't let it consume your day. When I was in the corporate world, I received 150 e-mails a day. Do the math. There's no way any human being can respond to that many e-mails a day and get the rest of the work done. Develop a system to keep up with them so they don't get out of control.

Respond to the most important e-mails first. (That should include e-mails from anyone directly involved with your paycheck—the boss, clients, etc.) People expect a reply within twenty-four hours. It's not always possible to respond that quickly, but do your best. If you don't have the information they need, reply anyway, to let them know you got their inquiry and you'll be back in touch. And if you're going to be out of your office for an extended period, consider putting an automatic response message on your e-mail.

6. *Include Your Contact Information at the Bottom of Every E-mail.*

You want to make it easy for people to get in touch with you. You never know when they might want to pick up the phone and have a live conversation. Include your name, title, company, address, phone numbers, and e-mail address.

7. *Don't Be a Coward and Deliver Bad News Via E-mail.*

If you have bad news to share with a colleague or a client, do it on the phone or face-to-face. Don't hide behind your computer to deliver the news. Do you want to open an e-mail and read bad news? Others don't either.

8. *Be Careful What You Forward.*

Let's say you've been having an internal e-mail conversation about a client issue. Once the issue is resolved, don't just forward the e-mail trail on to your client. Start with a new e-mail. The client doesn't need to see the internal conversation.

Never pass on inappropriate e-mails. You shouldn't use your business e-mail address to send jokes, chain letters, and so on. Tell your friends and family to send e-mails of that nature to your personal address.

9. Don't Hide Behind Your Computer.

Get up out of your chair and have a face-to-face conversation. You can't accomplish everything through e-mail. If an e-mail exchange is too long, it may save everyone time to have a live conversation.

10. Delete Does Not Mean Delete.

Just because you delete an e-mail doesn't mean a technology wizard can't find it. The good news is, if you accidentally deleted an important document, your friends in the IT department can find it. The bad news is, if you are sending or receiving inappropriate e-mails, they can find those, too.

11. E-mails Don't Always Make It to the Other End.

You would think (hope) your e-mails always make it to the recipients, but they don't. If you don't receive a response in a reasonable amount of time, call to confirm receipt of the e-mail.

Before You Hit the "Send" Button on an E-mail, Ask Yourself a Few Questions:

- Is the information clear? How's the tone?

- Is it professionally written, or is it a bit too casual?

- Are you sure it's appropriate to address this person by his or her first name? If not, use the surname. It's better to be formal than too casual.

- Did you include confidential information that should be communicated in person or on the phone?

- If you were reading the e-mail, would you "get it"?

- Did you check your spelling and grammar?

- Did you copy the right people on the e-mail?

THINK, THINK, THINK BEFORE YOU SPEAK

In college, your verbal communication style was probably fairly casual. When you start your career, you'll want to be sure you're communicating on a professional level. Be careful what you say. Words are powerful, and you can't take them back. Take a moment to think about what you're going to say before you open your mouth. Don't blurt out your first thought, especially if you're frustrated, confused, or unsure of the facts.

Sometimes fewer words are better. If you have a tendency to tell people how the clock is made when all they wanted was the time, consciously stop and think before you speak. For example, if you're on the elevator and the president of your organization asks, "How was your weekend?" you may be tempted to tell him *all* about your weekend. But the most appropriate response would be, "Great. How was yours?"

If you're tempted to say something negative about your company or one of your clients, resist the urge. You never know whom the person you're talking to knows.

Powerful Words to Use

"I'm sorry."

These words are difficult for some people to say. A good apology should be offered quickly, and it should be genuine. Never underestimate the power of saying you are sorry.

"We'll make it happen."

You want to be known as someone who gets the job done, someone who makes life easier for the team. If you say, "We'll make it happen" or "Consider it done," your colleagues and clients will love you.

"Please" and "Thank You."

This sounds obvious, but so many people never say these magical words. Somewhere along the way, we've gotten so busy that we forget to take the time to be courteous. Be the one who takes the time. Magical things can happen when you use simple words like "please" and "thank you."

"Do you have a minute?"

Before you launch into a conversation on the phone or in person, ask if it's a good time to talk. People will appreciate your giving them the opportunity to say it's not a good time right now but they'd love to visit later.

"I don't know."

Don't be afraid to say, "I don't know." If you don't know the answer, don't try to fake it. No one expects you to know everything. If someone asks you a question you can't answer, let him know you'll get the information and get back to him. Then follow through in a timely manner.

"I need help."

Asking for help is not a sign of weakness. You can't do this thing called life all by yourself. There's something inside us that says we need to prove to people we can do everything. Why?

If someone asks you to do something and you don't know how, ask for guidance. Consider saying something like, "I'd be more than happy to do it, I just need some additional information." If you're working on a big project and need help to meet your deadline, ask for help. That's what the team is there for. We're all in this together.

Words to Avoid

"That's not my job."

We're all on the same team, so it *is* your job. If someone asks you to do something and it's within your ability, do it. If it's not something you can do, help find someone who can.

"It's not my fault."

It may not technically be your fault, but those words send people over the edge. And, if it is your fault, remember those powerful words, "I take complete responsibility."

"I've paid my dues."

Many recent college graduates think that since they've earned their degree, they've already paid their dues. You won't want to hear this, but we never stop paying our dues. We should never think we're too good to do something. See everything as an opportunity.

"Hey, dude, what's your problem?"

A friend was training a twenty-five-year-old colleague on his new sales territory. Day after day, the new associate was late. When my friend called him one morning to see if he was on the way to the office, the trainee said, "Hey dude, what's your problem? I'll be there when I get there."

Say that to the wrong person at work, and you'll probably find yourself back on the job market.

Any words you wouldn't say around your precious grandmother.

I have seen some of the most able and talented people lose their effectiveness because of offensive language. If you use profanity at work, you'll lose the respect of your colleagues. People judge you by your language. Be careful with your words.

The next time you're about to use inappropriate language, think about your grandmother. If she were standing right there, would you say it?

IT'S ALL IN THE DELIVERY

Many times it's not what you say, but how you say it. Be aware of the tone of your e-mails, phone messages, and face-to-face conversations.

I had a speaking engagement at a hotel, and the audio-visual guy came by to check the microphone. He asked me if it was on, so I tapped the top of the microphone. He proceeded to give me a two-minute lecture, in front of my client, about why I shouldn't ever do that. I got his point after the first ten seconds, but he wouldn't let it go.

All he had to say was, "Did you know it's not good to tap the microphone? Just say a few words and I'll be able to tell if it's set right." Be sure you're not saying something that would embarrass someone. You wouldn't want them to do it to you. It's all in the delivery.

Let's say you submitted a proposal to your boss, a co-worker, or a client and you haven't heard back. Consider saying, "I know you are swamped right now. I just wanted to touch base with you to see if you'd had a chance to review the proposal I sent you. Please let me know if there's anything I can do to help. I'll look forward to hearing from you. Thanks."

That's as opposed to "Did you *ever* review the proposal I sent you? I've been waiting for two weeks and haven't heard from you."

Let's say one of your colleagues missed a deadline to give you a report you need. Consider saying, "Have you had a chance to finish the report?" As opposed to "Did you *ever* finish the report? The deadline was last week."

Feel the difference? Put yourself on the receiving end of this communication. Which one would immediately put you on the defensive?

The key to successful, effective communication is to think before you speak. Think about how you'd want someone to communicate with you. *What* you say and *how* you say it will have a lasting impact.

HOW'S YOUR TONE ON THE PHONE?

On the phone, tone of voice makes your first impression. People can't gauge your body language or look you in the eye. Your "hello" is the handshake that starts the conversation.

The Fine Art of Answering the Phone

It sounds so simple. The phone rings; you answer it. How hard can it be? Think about times you've called someone, and when they answered the phone, you felt as if you were an imposition. Or the tone in the other person's voice sounded as though she absolutely hated her job.

When you answer your phone, have a smile on your face and in your voice. You never know who might be calling. What if it's the chairman of your organization calling to invite you to a meeting? What if it's someone you met in the community calling to offer you a job? What if it's the client you've been pitching for the last six months?

If you have a negative tone in your voice, they'll wonder if that's the way you treat everyone. They'll wonder if that's the real you. Potential clients will wonder if you're only nice when you want their business.

You've spent your entire life answering the phone with a simple "hello," or perhaps something even more casual. Now that you're in the workplace, you'll need to answer by identifying yourself with at least your name. Pay attention to how your manager answers the phone. Include as much information as she does.

Just Because the Phone Rings Doesn't Mean You Have to Answer It

If you're rushing out of your office and your phone rings, don't answer it. If you don't have time to talk, it's going to make the conversation awkward for everyone.

If you're on deadline, don't get distracted by the phone. Don't answer it unless you can tell it's someone calling about the project, or if it's your boss. Resist the urge to answer the phone if someone is in your office. You want to give the person you're with your undivided attention. And you shouldn't put a person on hold to take another call, unless it's urgent.

Before you answer your phone, be sure you have the time to give the caller your full attention.

Random Phone Tips

Don't Hover.

Don't stand outside someone's door while she is on the phone and mouth something like, "We need you to review this by the end of the day." This happens all the time to one of my friends. One time, she was so distracted by the staff member standing in her doorway that she had to apologize to the caller *and* put him on hold so she could tell the staff member she'd get back to her later. It made for an awkward phone call and was inconsiderate of the staff member.

If your co-worker is on the phone, or it's obvious he's working on a big project, don't hover outside his office. Slip him a note asking him to call you, or come back later.

Lose the Speakerphone.

Speakerphones are annoying for the caller and the person receiving the call. People on the other end wonder how many people are listening in, and you sound like you're in a hole. Otherwise, they're great! Seriously, don't converse on a speakerphone unless you have to.

Are You Sure You're on Hold?

Don't say *anything* about a customer or client when you think you're on hold. You might not be. The same applies to the mute button on your phone. One time I called to check on a print job, and the woman who answered the phone thought I was on hold. She started screaming at her co-workers. I don't choose to do business with people who don't treat their employees with respect. As a result of her behavior, it was the last time I did business with her company.

Focus Before You Make the Call.

Don't dial the number until you're focused—not multitasking and responding to e-mails. Think about what you're going to say. Make some notes if you need to. When placing a call, make sure you have time to visit. You don't want to sound rushed, or the person you're calling isn't going to feel special. Be prepared for a live person to answer. It doesn't happen often, but it could.

Record Cheerfully.

Make sure you have a smile in your voice when you record your outgoing voice-mail message. Your greeting should include your name and department. Be sure to update your message if you're going to be out of the office for an extended period of time.

Call your number and listen to your message. How's the tone in your voice? Does it sound as if you were in a hurry when you recorded it? Does it sound as if you love your job, or does it sound as though work is the last place you want to be? Work may be the *last* place you want to be, but the caller doesn't need to know that.

Don't let your voice mailbox get full. It's frustrating to callers, and they may or may not call back. You never know what opportunity you may miss. And if your boss calls and can't leave you a message because your voice mailbox is full, you are *not* going to like what happens next.

In college, the outgoing message on your cell phone wasn't that important. It is now. Be sure it's professional and includes your full name. If you haven't updated your message since you graduated, do it right now. You never know who might call.

Leave Professional Voicemail Messages.

Make sure you have a smile in your voice when leaving a message. If you're trying to multitask, chances are you're going to get distracted. You may end up leaving a message you wish you could delete, but you can't.

Leave enough information to be helpful, but don't make it too long. I used to work with a woman who would leave three-minute voice-mail messages. How can anyone talk that long to a machine?

I've received messages in which the person just says, "Nancy, give me a call. We need to catch up." Oh, how I'd love to, but *who* are you? Always leave your name and number, even for someone you talk to frequently. There's a chance the person will be away from her office when she gets your message and may not have your number with her.

Return All Calls.

I'm stunned by the number of people who don't return calls. What if the phone call turned out to be from a prospective client who wanted to place a $100,000 order? You never know.

Telephone tag wastes so much time. Don't just leave a message saying, "This is Mark, returning your call." If you get voice mail, leave the information the other person asked for. And always leave your number, saying it slow enough for the person to write it down.

I received a message from a gentleman who said his number so fast I couldn't understand it. I could make out some of the numbers, but not all of them. I tried to return the call, but wasn't successful. He called back several times, and each time I was able to get one more number correct. I was finally able to piece together a phone number and return his call. Don't make someone have to work that hard. (I'm so glad I kept trying, because he wanted to make a large donation to The Dallas Morning News Charities.)

It's Not Your Personal Phone.

It's all right to place a personal call every now and then, but don't make a habit of it. The last thing you want is for your boss to walk by your office and hear you talking about what a great time you had while you were out with your friends last night.

YOUR LIFE IS A SERIES OF PRESENTATIONS

If standing before a group making a presentation terrifies you, you're in good company. It terrifies most people. You're going to spend the rest of your career making presentations, whether it's one-on-one or in front of a thousand people. Effective presentation skills distinguish successful professionals from everyone else. If you're going to be successful in your career (and you are), you need to get comfortable with public speaking.

I'll never forget the first big presentation I had to make in front of the entire management team. I thought I was going to die. I was *sure* they could hear my heart beating. The good news is I survived. So will you.

There are three keys to making great presentations: preparation, passion, and practice. Be sure to spend plenty of time preparing your remarks, whether it's for a staff meeting or a presentation at an industry conference. Let the audience feel your passion while you speak. And practice, practice, practice.

There will be times when you might trip a little during your presentation. Get over it. I've been speaking for over twenty-five years, and I still get tongue-tied every now and then. When it happens, recover as gracefully as you can, and keep going. If you don't make a big deal out of it, it won't be one.

The most embarrassing moment I ever had was early in my career. I was giving a presentation on freezing foods to a group of elderly women. (Keep in mind, they already knew more about freezing foods than I'll ever know.) When I got to the word "organism," I got tongue-tied. You probably already know the rest of the story. I tried and tried to say it correctly and just couldn't. These sweet little ladies giggled, and my face was as red as an apple.

After that experience, who would have *ever* thought I'd become a full-time motivational speaker? Remember the three P's of great presentation skills: preparation, passion, and practice.

BODY LANGUAGE—YOURS AND THEIRS

People can say a lot without saying a word. You need to be able to read someone's body language, because nonverbal communication is extremely important. There are times when people are saying one thing, but their body language is saying something else. Most of the time, body language speaks louder than words.

Test your ability to read body language. Rent a movie. Watch the first fifteen minutes of the movie without the sound, to see if you can figure out what is happening. Then watch it again to see how well you did.

I thought of this when I was on an airplane showing *The Devil Wears Prada*, starring Meryl Streep. Without earphones, it was obvious to me that this woman stepped on everyone on her way to the top of the fashion world. I found myself trying to figure out what was happening, without the benefit of the sound. Give it a try. It's an interesting exercise. Your ability to read body language is a powerful tool.

Your Body Language

If you're sitting in a meeting and you look bored out of your mind, you're not going to impress anyone. You may very well *be* bored out of your mind, but don't let others know you are.

If you're sitting there with your arms crossed, it sends the message you've turned people off. When I cross my arms, it's usually because I'm cold, but the other people in the room don't know that. So if I'm cold, I have to remind myself not to cross my arms so I don't send the wrong message. We have to be conscious of what *they're* thinking. Remember, it's all about them.

There are many professionals who have studied body language. I'm not an expert, but here's what I *do* know. People are not going to appreciate it if you do any of the following:

- Roll your eyes when they speak to you.

- Stare off into space, with your eyes glazed over.

- Drum your fingers on the desk or conference room table.

- Slouch in your chair.

People *will* appreciate it if you:

- Look them in the eye.

- Nod every once in a while so they'll know you're still with them.

- Sit up tall (but not too stiff). It shows confidence, alertness, and interest.

- Lean forward. It shows you're engaged in what's being said.

Smiling is one of the most positive gestures around. The lack of a smile can mean the exact opposite. If someone is generally positive and smiling, and then all of a sudden the smile goes away, you need to rewind your tape and think about what you might have said to change his body language.

Reading Body Language

If her body language says, "Don't say a word," then don't. If her body language says, "Speak up," then do. How will you know what someone's body language is saying? You have to pay close attention. You have to be able to read a face and interpret hand gestures. (Some hand gestures are *real* easy to figure out.)

If someone stands up while you're in his office, it's time to wrap up the conversation. If you're following someone to her car and she opens the door, she needs to go. If someone's walking into the bathroom, let him go.

The main objective is to be aware of the unspoken word. The more you observe, the better you'll get at reading body language.

DID YOU HEAR THAT?

How many times do you find your mind wandering when someone is talking to you? If you do, you're normal. Force yourself to stay focused. Look the other person in the eye and give her your undivided attention. Turn off those little voices in your head. If you're thinking about what you're going to say as the other person is talking, you're not listening.

Your ability to listen is key to your success. Good listening skills come naturally to some people, but most of us have to work at it. Some of the greatest misunderstandings in life come from miscommunication. You said one thing, and the other person heard something different.

Tune out distractions and focus on the conversation. Resist the urge to interrupt or jump in the second the other person pauses to take a breath. If you constantly interrupt people, you are going to wear them out. Over time, you may find fewer and fewer people who *want* to have a conversation with you.

Exceptional listening skills will help you stand above the crowd.

SURELY THEY KNOW

We all find ourselves thinking, "Surely they know." Your co-workers can't read your mind. They won't know unless you tell them.

"Surely they know I'm the perfect one to handle the project. I did something similar during an internship. It was on my resume." They *don't* necessarily know. There's a ninety-nine percent chance the last time they looked at your resume was during your interview. You'll need to bring it to their attention.

"Surely they know I have plans this weekend and can't work." How would they know? If you're asked to put in extra hours and already have plans, talk it over with your manager. There's a good chance she'll work with you to find another time to get the work done.

"Surely they know I can't take on one more assignment." There's no way for your colleagues to know everything you have on your plate. If someone asks you to take on an additional assignment, and you don't think there's any way you can do it, talk to him about it. Let him know what you're working on, and ask where the new project falls on the priority list.

Your ability to communicate is the key to your success. Looking for a promotion? Think you deserve a raise? Want to work on a special project? You won't know the answer until you ask. If you have something to say, speak up. Just be sure you're doing it in a respectful way.

CHAPTER SEVEN

Spinning Out of Control

◆

Think back to your college days when you were spinning out of control. There were days when you thought if you could just get organized, you could stay on top of your game. You may not be overwhelmed with work when you first start a job, but you will over time. Now is the time to develop great work habits and get your systems in place. Consider it an investment in your future.

Map Out a Plan

You need a road map, a plan that will help provide purpose and direction. It will help you stay focused and give you a vision for your future. Set goals and objectives for your projects, your career, and your life. They don't have to be elaborate. Just write down the steps you're going to take to achieve each goal.

Be sure your goals and objectives have a timeline, and are measurable. If it's a big goal or project, create manageable chunks. Otherwise, the whole thing will be so intimidating you won't know where to begin. That's when procrastination starts.

Each year, I develop a strategic plan for my business. I write down everything I want to accomplish, then set some "stretch goals." This is when I raise the bar and challenge myself to do more. I encourage you to do the same. We can always do more than we think we can.

Just be sure your expectations are realistic. Doing your best is one thing, but you don't want to set yourself up for failure by striving for the impossible. If you always set unrealistic expectations, you'll never experience the feeling of victory. All you'll feel is the agony of defeat.

I've seen numerous organizations over the years set unrealistic expectations, whether it's a fund-raising goal for a nonprofit organization or revenue goals for a Fortune 500 company. No matter what they did, it was never good enough.

If you set realistic expectations, while stretching a bit, you'll feel great at the end of the day. If you don't, you'll feel that no matter how hard you work, it's never enough. You want to set the bar high, but not too high.

ORGANIZATIONAL SAVVY

Your organizational skills are critical to your success. Chances are you'll be working for a company that's trying to do more with fewer people. If you're going to keep up with the workload, you're going to have to be organized.

If you're organized, you'll be more productive. If you're more productive, you'll meet more deadlines. If you meet more deadlines, you'll become known as a "go to" person. If you become a "go to" person, you'll have more opportunities. The more you do, the more you'll get to do, which will ultimately mean you'll have a great career.

If organization is not one of your strengths, get some help. Read books. Attend a training session. Consult with people who are well-organized. Ask them about their system and tips they can offer. Do *whatever* it takes to get organized. Organization systems are not "one size fits all." Take the information you gather and create a system that works for you.

You may not think this applies to you right now, especially if you've just started your job. However, one day the floodgates will open, and you'll be swamped just like everyone else on the team. Develop a system now, before you need it.

You'll Know You're Organized When:

- You can find the information you or your colleague needs in five minutes or less.

- You never miss a deadline.

- The only things on your desk are the projects you're working on today.

- You can put your hands on the business card of the person you met last month.

Tips for Staying Organized

Get a Calendar.

It's possible you got through your college years without a calendar. I'm not sure how you did, but I've had plenty of recent college graduates tell me they never had one.

You might think you don't need a calendar because you can remember everything. You might be able to keep up with everything on your first day of work, when there's nothing on your calendar. After day one, you're going to need one. Even if you don't think you need it, get one. It'll make your boss nervous if you don't have a calendar.

Have Master and Daily "To Do" Lists.

Your master "to do" list will be a comprehensive list of *everything* you need or want to do. Include everything, and I mean everything. You don't want to lose any of your great ideas. Take fifteen minutes at the end of every day to prepare a "to do" list for tomorrow. This will come from your master list, along with any new assignments you received today.

Evaluate the items on your list, and then prioritize them. Select the three most important things. When you get in the office, make yourself do those three things before you do anything else. (OK, you can get your coffee first.) After you tackle those three, cross them off your list, so you'll have a feeling of accomplishment. Then, identify the next three and keep the process going.

The key is to keep your "to do" list in front of you all day long. Refer to it several times a day. If you haven't done anything on the list and it's lunch time, you'll need to focus when you get back to the office.

Everything takes longer than you think it will. If you think it will take an hour to complete a project, block off two hours on your calendar. If you overestimate the time you'll need, you could be left with a moment of peace. Also, allow time in your day for unexpected crises. Don't schedule your day so tightly you leave the office frustrated because you didn't get anything on your list done.

Schedule Time for You.

Block off time on your calendar to get your work done. I wished I'd learned this a long, long time ago. When I was in the corporate world, I spent six to seven hours a day in meetings. That doesn't leave much time to get the work done—returning phone calls, answering e-mails, working on projects, etc.

I was bad about scheduling every minute of my day for the people who wanted to meet with me. I eventually figured out I needed to block off time on my calendar to finish the things on my "to do" list. It made all the difference in the world.

Schedule Follow-Up Time.

If you ask someone who's been working for a while why he seems so out of control, he'll probably tell you it's because he never has time to follow up on commitments he's made. After you attend a meeting, go straight to your office and summarize your notes while they are fresh in your mind. If you came away with some assignments, put them on your "to do" list. This simple step will help you stay on task and meet your deadlines. And hopefully, it will keep you from getting out of control.

Fix the Things That Drive You Crazy.

What bugs you? Is your telephone cord too short? Don't have enough filing space? Is your computer too slow?

Make a list of the things that drive you crazy and fix them. If they're things you can take care of on your own, great. If they require an expenditure that needs to be approved, go to your boss with your list. If you tell him you could be more productive if the things on your list were resolved, chances are he'll help you. It's amazing how taking care of the little things that drive us crazy can make our lives happier and improve our productivity.

Clear the Clutter, Clear the Mind.

There aren't many people who can operate at their peak if their desk is a mess. If you find you're spending more time *looking* for the work you need to do than *doing* the work, you need to take the time to get organized.

If you work with a Type A personality, your messy desk is going to make that person nervous. What if your boss walks by your office and sees your messy desk? Now she may hesitate to give you an exciting new project because she doesn't think you could handle the extra work, based on the work she saw stacked on your desk.

Or what if a client drops by unexpectedly? He walks in your office and sees your messy desk, then walks out wondering if you're going to be able to handle the big order he was about to place. It could happen.

What's in Those Stacks?

The community services team at *The Dallas Morning News* and WFAA-TV used to call it the "train wreck theory." If someone on the team got hit by a train, could we do that person's job? If something happens to you, your co-workers need to be able to do your job. Or if you're out of the office and need something, they need to be able to find it for you. You may know what's in those stacks, but will your colleagues?

Expect the Unexpected.

If you're on top of your game, you'll be able to handle unexpected projects (opportunities). But if you are constantly living on the edge and running behind, you'll just be frustrated when someone gives you a new project.

Things will go wrong, so build in extra time to deal with the unexpected. And if something unexpected comes along, like floor tickets to a concert, you'll be able to take advantage of the opportunity.

Out of Control—Plan a Vacation. (I'm Serious.)

Something amazing happens to our productivity level when we know we're going to be out of the office for a few days. Somehow, we find a way to get all those things on our "to do" list done. Try it. You'll get caught up and you'll be headed somewhere fun for a couple of days. When you get back from vacation, try to keep things in order. You'll be glad you did.

DEADLINES—MEET THEM OR BEAT THEM

I'm convinced nothing would get done if it weren't for deadlines. I like to think of deadlines as the motivation we need to stay on task.

It's always better to under-promise and over-deliver. If you *think* you can complete a project by Wednesday, but you're *sure* you can do it by Friday, tell them you'll have it ready by Friday. If you say you're going to do something, do it. You want to be known as someone who follows through on commitments.

Your bosses believe in you and trust you'll do what you say you'll do. The first time you don't, they'll excuse you. Or at least some bosses will. The second time, they'll start to wonder if you can keep your commitments. If it continues to happen, they'll stop giving you projects. They don't have time to teach you the importance of commitment.

The last thing you want to do is receive a call from your boss or your client telling you about a missed deadline. I worked for a guy who had the best tickler system in the world. (A tickler system is a dated filing system which helps you keep track of projects and deadlines.) One time, he had to remind me about an important deadline I had missed. That was the last time I ever wanted that to happen. He had much more important things to do than remind me of my deadline.

If the publisher of a major daily newspaper could keep up with his own deadlines, as well as those of everyone who worked for him, *surely* I could keep up with mine. Make sure your tickler system is a good one.

Many years ago, I had a big project due by 3 p.m. on a Friday. I busted my butt to get the project completed on time, and when I went to my boss' office to give it to him, he wasn't there. I asked the receptionist where he was. She informed me he was gone for the day. I immediately said some things to her that in hindsight I shouldn't have said. On Monday, she shared my inappropriate comments with my boss. You know where this story is going. He was not pleased with me.

I learned a valuable lesson that day: If your boss gives you a deadline, just meet it. Take pride in knowing you did what you were asked to do. A second lesson I learned: Never, ever say bad things about your boss to a fellow employee. It'll come back and bite you every time.

If You're Going to Miss a Deadline, Let the Person Know

Chances are your deadline is related to another deadline. Missing yours is probably going to cause a domino effect. You miss yours, which means she'll have to miss hers. People generally understand if you let them know, so they can plan accordingly.

If you're going to miss a deadline because you're waiting for information from someone else, you have a couple of options. You could turn in the work with a note stating, "Additional information to come from Jordan." Or, you could send an e-mail to the person who's expecting the report and say something like, "We're still waiting on a piece of information from Jordan. Would you like me to turn in what I have, or would you prefer we wait until we have all the information you requested?"

The key is you didn't say anything negative about Jordan. You just stated that you didn't have his information. This is a whole lot better than saying, "Jordan has not responded to multiple requests for the information. He obviously doesn't understand how important this project is to you. Blah, blah, blah." Feel the difference?

Do your best to meet deadlines or beat them. If you continue to miss deadlines, you won't be trusted with bigger responsibilities.

Do the Most Important Thing Now

You may have twenty things on your "to do" list. If you're going to meet deadlines, you're going to have to prioritize. The tendency is to do the easy things first, so you can feel a sense of accomplishment. But if you do that, you may not be doing the most important things.

Before you do anything on your list, ask yourself, "Is this the most important thing I need to do right now?" If you can get the most important things done, it'll make you feel great. Then you can breeze through the rest of your list.

MULTITASK WITH CAUTION

Multitasking will fry your brain. Trust me, I know. There are days when I feel exhausted from trying to do too many things at one time. We have to multitask to a certain degree to keep up with the workload. However, be aware of the challenges that come with multitasking. If you're trying to do too many things at once, you won't be doing your best work. And you might say something you didn't mean to say, because you didn't take the time to think first.

If you're filing something while you're on the phone, the caller isn't getting your undivided attention. Making the person on the phone feel special is more important than putting the file away. And there's a good chance you won't remember later where you put the file, because you weren't focused when you put it away. If you're trying to respond to e-mails while someone is at your desk asking you a question, the person isn't going to feel valued.

The ability to handle multiple tasks or projects effectively is key to your success, but proceed with caution.

PROCRASTINATION CAUSES PAIN

Do you tend to procrastinate? Be honest.

I've done my fair share of procrastinating over the years, and here's what I've learned—it's not worth it. Have you ever thought about how much mental energy we waste *thinking* about what we need to do? It would have taken less time and less mental energy if we just did it.

If you're a procrastinator, try to figure out why. Do you avoid projects that take a lot of time? Or the ones where you don't have all the information you need to get started? Are you putting it off because you don't think you have the time to make it perfect?

Procrastination is a survival mechanism to avoid something we fear. The irony is the fear actually builds the longer we procrastinate. So putting it off makes things worse. Make a list of all the things you've been putting off. Prioritize the list and do them, one by one. You'll sleep better at night.

It's easy to procrastinate on projects that are so big we don't have a clue where to start. If you're assigned a big project, break it down into manageable chunks, so you won't be overwhelmed by the size of it. Set intermediate deadlines, and you'll have a better chance of getting the project completed on time.

If you're having trouble focusing, change the scenery. Take your work to a conference room where it's quiet and you can concentrate. Go to a coffee shop. Ask your boss if you can take the project home to work on it. Do whatever it takes to focus on what's most important at the moment.

Procrastination leaves little time for the unexpected—the computer developing an attitude, the printer running out of ink, realizing at the last minute that you don't have some important information to complete the report. Or what if you get invited to something special and have to decline because you've procrastinated on a big project? Give yourself some breathing room.

STRESSFUL TIMES

Work can be stressful, but I'm convinced most of our stress is self-induced. Stay with me and you'll see what I mean.

We get stressed because we want everything to be perfect. No one told us that we had to be perfect. That's something we decided. We get stressed over the amount of work our employers ask us to do. We worry about whether we're being as productive as we could be. But what if our workload is unrealistic? Do we take the time to tell our bosses, or do we just agonize over it?

We lose sleep thinking about promotions others received. Instead of thinking about what we *didn't* get, we should focus on what we need to do to get the next one.

We get stressed over something we said or didn't say. I remember a time when I couldn't stop thinking about something inappropriate I said in a meeting with my boss. I worried about it for days and finally decided to talk him to clarify what I meant to say. A few minutes into my explanation, he asked, "What are you talking about?" I'd spent days worrying about something that was not a big deal.

Make a list of all the things stressing you out. How many of them can you control? Do what you can to change the things you can control. For the ones that others control, sit down and talk to them. Together, you might be able to come up with some solutions. You won't know until you have the conversation.

There will still be things on your list, but now the list is shorter, and you should be able to deal with what's left. The next time you're feeling overwhelmed, take a look at what's going on. See if it's stress you're creating on your own; then do something about it.

IS IT EVER GOOD ENOUGH?

It's great that you want to set high standards for the work you do. But you don't have to be perfect all the time. Perfectionism is a self-induced stressor.

I spent the first twenty-five years of my life trying to please my dad. He was a wonderful man, but he was also a perfectionist. It seemed like no matter what I did, it wasn't good enough. I would mow the lawn, and he would mow over it. I would help him wash the car, and he would find the one spot I missed.

Over the years, I realized things didn't have to be perfect to be good enough. I also realized my dad was very pleased with the way I lived my life and with what I had accomplished. He just had a hard time showing it.

Throughout your life, you've heard people say, "Just do your best. That's all we can expect of you." This also applies to your career. You don't have to be perfect to have a successful career; just do your very best.

CHAPTER EIGHT

BOSSES: THE GOOD, THE BAD, AND THE UGLY

I've seen them all—the good, the bad, and the ugly. I *wish* I could tell you every boss you'll ever have will be wonderful. But I can't. Along the way, you'll have some great bosses. You may also encounter some bad ones.

Everyone has a different opinion of what makes a good boss. For me, a good boss is someone I respect and can learn from. Someone who empowers the team to do the job and holds the team to high standards. A good boss is quick to respond to the needs of the team and celebrates successes on a regular basis.

They're good communicators, who are out in front carrying the banner, rather than walking behind the team with a whip. They glorify team spirit, seeing the members of their team as partners. When a good boss introduces someone, she says, "We work together," rather than "He works for me."

Good bosses hire people who are smarter than they are. (That's why they hired you.) They trust the team and have a humble spirit. They use their hearts as well as their heads.

A bad boss is someone who is slow to act on things. Someone who micromanages. Someone who doesn't give much direction and takes forever to make a decision. Bad bosses take credit for everything. They are cold and insensitive, have anger outbursts, and bark commands. You never know what you're going to get, due to their mood swings.

In defense of the bad ones, here's one of the reasons why they turn out that way. Many times in business, we take great employees and promote them to management. We think just because they were great at their original jobs, they'll be great managers. Then, many times, we don't give them any training on how to be great bosses. We just put them in management positions and assume they'll know what to do.

And for the bosses who are downright ugly—I feel sorry for them. I've seen some of the most arrogant, self-centered people in the world—managers who lose their tempers and say things you wouldn't dream of saying in the workplace. I've seen them humiliate their staffs in front of others. These people are just downright mean.

I wonder how they live with themselves. I wonder if they treat their families the same way they treat their colleagues. Don't spend a lot of time wondering how they got that way. We'll never know. Just focus on you, and remember to always take the high road.

The good news is that I haven't seen many ugly bosses. And the other piece of good news is that their behavior usually catches up with them. Most of the ugly ones I've seen along the way aren't around anymore.

On your journey, I hope you encounter only the good ones. But the reality is you may see some bad ones. There's a good reason why you'll have some bad bosses: You'll learn all the things *not* to do when you're the boss, and you'll have a deep appreciation for all the good bosses.

The Scoop About Bosses

There are four things you need to know about bosses.

- *No two bosses are the same.*
  That's the good news *and* the bad news.

- *Everyone has a boss.*
  Your boss has a boss too, so don't think you're the only one that's dealing with bosses.

- *Bosses are people, just like you.*
  Why are we intimidated by the boss? It seems like the bigger the title, the higher the intimidation factor. There's no need to be intimidated by them; they're just people. If he was your best friend's dad, would you be intimidated by him? Probably not. You should treat your boss with respect, but that doesn't mean he should intimidate you.

- *You don't get to choose your bosses; they choose you.*
  While it's true they choose you, I encourage you to ask your boss some questions during the interviewing process, to make sure she's someone you'd enjoy working with.

Managing Your Manager

The relationship you have with your boss is critical. It's your responsibility to manage the relationship with your manager. You may be thinking, "You have *got* to be kidding." I'm not.

Here's why you need to be the one to manage this partnership. Your boss has numerous responsibilities. Many of them you won't even be aware of. But there's only one of you. Your boss probably has multiple direct reports, and no telling how many bosses he's trying to keep happy. If you focus on keeping your boss happy, he can focus on keeping his boss happy, and you both win.

If you focus on making your manager's life easier, you're going to have an amazing career. You *want* to have a great relationship with your bosses. You want to be the one they can count on, no matter what.

Tips for Making the Most of the Partnership

Respect Your Manager's Time.

Everyone is busy. You're busy, and your boss is busy. Being your boss is just one of her many responsibilities. Don't demand too much of her energy. She expects you to handle the details and make decisions on your own.

Look for Ways to Make Their Lives Easier.

Remember, it's all about them. Make their lives easier. Put yourself in their shoes. When you're the boss, won't you want a team of people who make your life easier?

Find out what's important to your boss; then figure out what you can do to help. If you know what's important to your manager, it will help you focus your time and energy on those priorities.

I had an incredible team when I worked for *The Dallas Morning News* and WFAA-TV. They could do anything I could do. Most of the time they could do things better. When they would ask what they could do to help me, there were times I was so covered up with projects for my bosses I couldn't stop long enough to think about what they could take off my plate. But I always loved the fact that they offered to help.

Ask your manager what you can do to help. If she doesn't give you something right away, it's not because she doesn't need or want your help. When she comes up for air, she'll think about how you can make her life easier.

Give Your Bosses Positive Feedback.

Let them know how much you appreciate them. Don't think of it as sucking up to your boss. Think of it as one person saying something positive to another person. Remember, the one thing we have in common is that we're all human beings.

And after you've had a chance to develop a trusting relationship with your boss, give him some constructive feedback. We're all in this together, so if you see something he could do different or better, tell him.

When I was in the corporate world, some of the best ideas came from members of our team. I had a demanding job and worked long hours. (A choice I made because I loved my job so much.) Someone would come to me and say, "Nancy, have you considered doing . . . ?" Every suggestion they made was a great one and much appreciated.

Make Them Look Good.

Your life will be so awesome if you understand the importance of making your boss look good. If you make your boss look good, it makes *you* look good. Help your manager move to the next level; it may mean you move up with her.

Remember the "No Surprise" Rule.

Keep your boss informed. The last thing you want is to have your boss find out something critical from someone else. You shouldn't *ever* put him in a situation where he's sitting in a meeting and learns something about his department for the first time. It's your responsibility to make sure your boss has all the information he needs.

Don't wait until something becomes a crisis before you give your manager an update. If you discuss it early, it's less likely to reach crisis mode.

Got a Problem—Offer a Solution.

Bosses make a million decisions every day. They can't be the ones to figure out everything. That's why they have you. If you want to be a shining star in your organization, offer a solution to challenges that come along. (As I mentioned earlier, I say "challenges" because I don't like the word "problem.")

If an issue needs to be addressed, try saying something like, "I've been thinking about (the challenge), and I have an idea. What would you think if . . . ?" Your boss will love the fact that you took the time to propose a solution. Then together you can resolve the issue. If you have several options to propose, be sure you've thought about the pros and cons of each solution, so you'll be prepared for a productive discussion.

Stay Two Steps Ahead.

If you can anticipate your bosses' needs, you're going to have an amazing career. Bosses love that.

The community services team was always two steps ahead of me. I'd call to ask them to prepare some detailed information for a report I needed for my boss, and they'd say, "We've already prepared the information. Shall we bring it into your office now?" Oh, how I loved them. They always made us look good.

Support Your Manager's Decisions.

It's your job to support decisions made by the management team of your organization. I didn't say you had to agree with them, but you do need to support them. As much as you'll want to understand why some decisions are made, you won't be able to. You can't know everything that went into a particular decision. Trust the leadership of your organization.

"Can You Come to My Office?"

When the boss calls and says those words, we all panic. We immediately wonder what we did wrong. Why do we *always* think it's going to be bad news? It's human nature; we all do it. Think positive thoughts. She might be calling you in to tell you about your promotion. You never know.

When your boss asks you to come to her office, just walk in there with a notepad, your calendar, and a positive attitude. And remember to breathe.

Timing Is Everything.

You need to carefully consider how, when, and where to bring a new idea to your boss. If he's busy, not having a good day, or in a bad mood, chances are he'll say no.

If you want to talk to your boss about a raise, a promotion, or taking vacation during the busiest time of the year, you want to wait until the time is right. It'll bring back memories of when you were younger and had to wait until your parents were in the right mood to improve the chances of getting the response you wanted.

The same is true with your boss. Just because it's at the top of your urgent list, doesn't mean now is the best time to pop the question. Timing is everything.

Dumping or Delegating?

There will be days when your boss gives you an assignment and you'll feel like you've been dumped on. A number of twentysomethings have told me they feel that way. Never think of it as dumping. You want to work for someone who delegates, because it means they trust you and know you'll get the work done.

If I had a project for a member of our team, I could call her and say, "Can you come into my office? I have an opportunity for you." They knew me well enough to know I was about to assign them a big project. They always came to my office with a great attitude, because they saw everything as an opportunity. There may be days you feel like you've been dumped on, but actually you've just been given a great opportunity.

TEN THINGS THAT WILL DRIVE YOUR BOSS CRAZY

Every manager has a list of pet peeves. You should avoid doing anything you know is going to drive your boss nuts. Oh sure, there are days when it would be fun to do something to send him or her over the edge. But if you want to have a successful career, I wouldn't go there.

Here's a short list of things you'll want to avoid. You'll want to ask your boss what drives her crazy, so you can have a complete list of things *not to do.*

1. *Arguing About Things You've Been Asked to Do.*

You may have been able to argue a bit with your parents or a professor, but I don't know many bosses who encourage their employees to argue with them. If you're constantly negotiating or constantly asking, "Why, why, why?" you're going to wear your boss out.

Then your boss might start wearing you out, and you won't like it. It's OK to ask why, just don't make it a debate.

2. *Not Taking Notes.*

If you don't take notes, your boss will wonder if you're going to be able to remember everything discussed. Even if you think you'll remember, you may not. Taking notes gives the impression you're interested in what's being said. If someone says something and you write it down, you're signaling what that person said was important. This applies to your boss, clients, and colleagues.

As you move along in your career and have more and more information to keep up with, you'll have to write things down to keep up. Taking notes is a good practice to start before you get overloaded with things to remember.

There's one exception: There may be times when your boss doesn't want you to take notes because she is sharing confidential information with you. She'll let you know.

3. *Arriving Late and Leaving Early.*

If you care about your professional success (and I know you do), don't get to work late or leave early on a regular basis.

Your employer is counting on you to be at work. If you're not, it makes it hard to get all the work done. If your boss can't count on you to be there, he will have no choice but to assign key projects to other members of the team—something you don't want to happen.

Sometimes, you won't be able to go to work. You may be sick, a family emergency may arise, or you may have some other valid reason. If you can't make it to the office, or you're going to be late, be sure to call and let the boss know, so she can plan accordingly.

A friend of mine hired a new college grad. One day, about a month after the employee started work, he didn't show up. My friend started getting worried, so she called him at home. When the employee answered the phone, he said, "Oh, I didn't think to call you." The good news is that his boss gave him another chance. Be courteous and responsible. Let your boss know if you won't be in the office.

4. *Going over Their Heads.*

Be careful, because you're walking on thin ice. Try your best to work it out before you decide you need to take an issue to the next level. Chances are good your manager's boss is going to support him, not you. Put yourself in the other person's shoes. If someone went over your head, wouldn't you want your boss to stand by your side? Sure you would.

If you decide you have to discuss an issue with upper management, be sure you've done your homework. You won't want to come off as a whiner. Focus on the facts of the situation, rather than on personality conflicts. Focus on issues upper management cares about—project delays, damage to relationships with clients, potential lost revenue, or unethical behavior.

Keep in mind, even if you've done your homework, upper management may still support your boss. If that's the case, just walk away and know you've done everything you can to bring an important situation to their attention. Then drop it. Over time, you'll have to decide if the issue is important enough to cause you to move on.

5. *Constant Interruptions.*

Do interruptions drive you crazy? Every time we're interrupted, it pulls us away from what we are focused on. It may take a long time to refocus.

If you constantly interrupt your boss with one question at a time, you're going to drive her nuts. Put yourself in her shoes. If you were sitting in your office working on a big project, and every five minutes someone interrupted you, wouldn't you be frustrated?

Schedule a convenient time to meet with your manager. List everything you want to discuss, and prioritize the list, so the most important things get covered. Take an extra copy of the list with you, in case the manager wants one. If you run out of time, you can schedule a follow-up meeting or send an e-mail with additional questions. One day, when you're the boss, you'll want a team who does this for you.

6. *Copying Your Boss on Every E-mail You Send.*

Only copy your boss on e-mails he needs to see. Use your good judgment. I've seen people over the years who copy their bosses on almost every e-mail they send, so their bosses would know how much work they're doing. Do you think those employees might have an insecurity issue?

Bosses don't have time to read every detail of everything you're working on. They expect you to handle the details and keep them informed on the most important things.

7. *Telling, Not Asking.*

If you want to take some vacation time or leave early on Friday, just ask. Chances are your boss will accommodate your request. However, if you walk in and *announce* you're talking off early, it won't sit very well.

8. *Not Following Directions.*

If your boss gives you specific directions, follow them. A good friend, who's a partner in his law firm, told me a story about a young associate who wouldn't follow strict instructions.

The associate repeatedly sent information directly to clients, without authorization or approval from the partners. After the third time, the partners began to believe he was either deceitful or just not very smart. My friend explained to the young associate that neither was good for him. He wasn't with the firm long.

9. B*eing a Clock Watcher.*

I'm a *big* believer in balance. I don't think people should work extremely long hours, but there are some managers who will go nuts if you leave your office every single day at 5 p.m. They need to see you there "after hours" every once in a while.

10. *Abusing Technology at Work.*

I hear lots of complaints from managers who have recent college graduates sitting at their computers, instant messaging their friends. This is going to drive your boss crazy. And while you may be tempted to surf the Internet while you're at work, don't. Your computer is company property and should be used only for company-related business.

CHAPTER NINE

RELATIONSHIPS:
TO HAVE AND TO HOLD

———◆———

One of the most important things you'll do in life is build and nurture relationships. At this point in your life, relationships are extremely important to you. Why? Because you are beginning to build a network that will be a part of your life forever. It may be a relationship that opens a door for you to land your first job.

When I talk to college graduates about their careers, I always encourage them to let every adult in their lives know what their career goals are. Many times they say, "Oh, no. I'm *not* going to let my mom or dad help me get a job. I'm going to do this on my own." *Why* would you try to do it on your own, when you have so many people who love you and want you to succeed?

Think about it this way—the adults in your life have spent years and years developing relationships. They can help you in a big way at this critical time in your life. Let them help. They're not going to *get* you the job; they'll just be opening some doors for you.

My whole career has been based on relationships. My first job out of college came from a relationship I had with my best friend's dad. My next job was based on a relationship I had with someone I knew from being involved in the community. Being promoted to vice president was based on a relationship I developed with the publisher. And every success I've had in my own business has been built on a relationship.

I'm living proof that building and nurturing relationships is the key to your success. Relationships are everything. Cherish and nurture *all* of them.

WHAT'S IN A NAME?

Are you good at remembering people's names? If so, congratulations! If not, you're in good company. Most people are challenged when it comes to remembering names.

When you call people by their names, you'll have an immediate personal connection with them. People love to hear their names. Use names a lot, but not too much. Overdo it, and people will think you went to a seminar to learn that technique.

Address people in a formal way, until they give you permission to call them by their first names, especially if you're on the phone or addressing a letter or e-mail. If you're face-to-face and you feel comfortable using their first names, go for it. But it's always safer to start with Mr. or Ms.

Be sure to get names right. If someone introduces himself as Thomas Allen, never assume he goes by Tom. If a business card or e-mail signature line uses a formal name, use that until you are told otherwise. What do you do if someone gets your name wrong? Gently correct the person when the time is right. Be sure to do it in way that's not embarrassing.

When you meet someone, always say, "It's great to *see* you," rather than "It's great to *meet* you." Here's why: If you say, "It's great to meet you," and you've already met the person and just can't remember, you're embarrassed. "It's great to see you" works, whether you've met the person before or not.

Tips for Remembering Names

There's a lot happening when you meet someone for the first time. You're shaking hands, smiling, looking the person in the eye, *and* trying to introduce yourself.

You have to be totally focused. As soon as the person says his or her name, repeat it. "Elizabeth, it's great to see you." If you listen to her name, then say the name out loud, you've doubled your chance of being able to remember it. If you didn't catch it, say, "I'm sorry. Could you say your name again?" Then say it out loud. Give the person one of your business cards, and ask for one of hers. If she doesn't have one with her, write her name down as soon as you can.

This has happened to all of us: Someone walks up to you, greets you by name, and talks at length about how great it is to see you. And you don't have a *clue* who it is. Or the face is familiar, but the name completely escapes you. This situation can be embarrassing, but it can be handled with tact and grace.

Let the person know you're glad to see him, too. One way of refreshing your memory is to ask what's been going on since you last saw him. His response may reveal something that will trigger your memory. If you're lucky, you'll even remember his name.

If you still can't remember, you have two options. You can say, "I apologize. I'm drawing a blank on your name." Or you can ask for a business card. Say something like, "I'd love to have one of your cards, so I can be sure I have all your current contact information."

Here's the key—focus, repeat, and write it down. If you do that every time you meet someone, you'll become a master at remembering names.

CARRY BUSINESS CARDS 24/7

As you meet more and more people, you'll want to be sure you carry business cards with you at *all* times. Your cards are one of the best marketing tools you have. In order to make it easy for people to do business with you, you have to make it easy for people to find you. If you're still looking for your first job, get some business cards made. You want to make it easy for potential employers to have your contact information.

I am always amazed at the number of people who don't carry business cards. I've heard every excuse in the book.

Women are the worst. It's always a challenge for a woman to find a business card in her purse. Why do we have to carry so much junk? We pull out our billfold, our makeup bag, our brush, and we keep saying, "I *know* I have a business card in here somewhere." Invest in a business card holder, and always keep it in your purse.

If a woman doesn't have a business card with her, it's probably because she changed purses. Put a few business cards in every purse, and you'll be ready to go to the next event.

If you know you're about to enter a room where you're going to need business cards, put your card holder on top of all your other stuff before you go into the room. Or better yet, wear something that has pockets and just put a handful of cards in your pocket.

Guys, you are pretty bad, too. You either don't have business cards with you, or the ones you have look as if they've been in your billfold forever.

One time, I had a guy completely unload his billfold to find a business card. He pulled out his credit cards, his driver's license, and pictures of his kids. Then he finally found one poor little card. He looked at the front of it, then turned it over to see if there was anything written on the back. And there was—a phone number.

I could see his mind working trying to remember whose number it was. He finally figured it out, handed me the card, and said, "That's OK, you can have this one. I don't need that number anymore."

Unbelievable! You know what it made me want to do? Call the number on the back of his card. He should have said, "I'll be happy to mail you one of my business cards," then mailed it to me within twenty-four hours.

If you're going out in public, and you might meet someone— which is every time you're in public—put some business cards in your pocket. You never know whom you might see.

What Do You Do with the Business Cards You Collect?

Every time you receive a business card, it can be the beginning of a wonderful relationship. Make a note on the back of the card show- ing where you met the person; date the card and file it. Don't just put the cards in a drawer somewhere. Develop a system. File them. Organize them. Enter the information in your contacts database.

When I first started my career, I began collecting business cards. Over the years, I've had the opportunity to meet a lot of wonderful people. My colleagues were always surprised by what they called my "million-dollar Rolodex." I had seven Rolodexes and could tell you a story about every person represented. You will have an opportunity to meet some terrific people along the way. Be sure you create a system to keep in touch with them.

I always say relationships are everything. You need to cherish and nurture every relationship. When you meet new people, realize that someday they might need you, or you might need them. They could become your new best friends. Getting their business cards is the first step to developing relationships that will last a lifetime.

Building Strong, Lasting Relationships

One of the best ways to develop relationships is to attend events in the community. Get out and meet people. Everyone you meet could become a new client or your new employer. Whether you're attending a business function or a networking event, these tips will help you build strong, lasting relationships.

Prepare an "Elevator Speech."

When someone says, "Tell me about you," what are you going to say? Write a summary of what you want people to know that can be delivered in thirty seconds or less, the length of an average elevator ride. Make it upbeat and succinct. If you give them more than thirty seconds worth, you run the risk of turning them off. They'll wonder if you're going to be doing the talking the whole time. Make it short and memorable.

It All Begins with "Hello."

Walking into a room full of strangers is intimidating for everyone. You don't have to wait for people to walk up to you—go to them. If you see someone standing by herself, she's probably as nervous as you are. She'll be relieved you started the conversation.

When you approach someone, be genuine, positive, and personable. Smile, introduce yourself, and you're on your way. If you see someone you want to meet and no one has taken the time to introduce you, why not introduce yourself? It's a scary thought for a lot of people, but it's not that hard. It all begins with "hello."

Show Genuine Interest in Others.

Focus on them, not on you. Ask them to tell you about themselves. (Hopefully, they have an elevator speech.) Listen to what they have to say. Your goal is to form a personal connection. Be genuinely interested in hearing about their careers, their families, their passions, and anything else they want to share with you.

Make it *all* about them. Focus the conversation on how you can help them, not what they can do for you. You'll build a rapport with them and they'll always remember how special you made them feel.

How Do You Join Conversations in Progress?

If you see someone you want to visit with in a group of people who are already in a conversation, stand outside their circle. Stand so they can see you out of the corners of their eyes. They'll eventually break the conversation and invite you to join the group.

If the person you want to talk to doesn't see you, you have two options. You can either walk away and catch him later, or you can gently touch the back of his arm to get his attention.

Don't interrupt a conversation to get someone's attention. I've seen so many people over the years walk up to a group of people who are talking and say, "I don't mean to interrupt." Then they jump right in and start a new conversation. It's awkward for everyone.

Don't Sit with the People You Already Know.

I'm always surprised by the number of people who attend events in the community and sit with the people they work with. When you attend a networking event, one of the goals is to meet new people. You can visit with the people you know, but don't sit with them the entire time.

What Do You Do if You're Ready to End a Conversation?

This one is always a little tricky. You may have just met someone who has a lot to say, and it doesn't appear the person is going to stop talking anytime soon. How can you walk away gracefully?

One approach is to say, "It was such a pleasure visiting with you. I don't want to monopolize your time. I know you want to visit with other people." Or consider saying, "I enjoyed meeting you. There are a few other people I wanted to catch before they leave. I hope our paths cross again." Then smile and move on.

Always Make People Feel Comfortable.

Promise me you'll never walk up to someone and say, "You don't remember me, do you?" *Why* would anyone say that? The person either remembers you or she doesn't. If she doesn't, it's going to be awkward for everyone.

I always reintroduce myself. I'm good with names, but I realize some people aren't, so I try to make it easy for them. You always want to make people feel comfortable.

Observe How Others Work a Room.

If someone you work with is good at relationship building, watch what that person does. Learn from her. Ask if she'd be willing to take you along to a few events, so you can watch her in action. Building relationships is easier than you might think. It just takes practice.

Wear a Nametag.

If you go to an event and they have nametags, wear one. You may be good with names, but others may not be. Your nametag helps them if their brains freeze when you walk up to them. Here's a little nametag trick: Always place it on your right shoulder. It makes it easy for someone to read when the two of you are shaking hands.

Follow Up.

After you meet someone new, send a personal note letting the person know how much you enjoyed meeting him. Very few people follow up with a note, so when you do, he'll always remember you.

Keep Doing It.

The more you get out and meet new people, the easier it will be. I've been building relationships for a long time, and there are times when it's hard, even for me, to walk into a room where I don't know a soul. After the first "hello," the rest is easy. There will be times when you don't want to go to a function. Every time I've ever felt that way, I was always glad I went to the event. Wonderful things can't happen if you choose to stay home. Just go—you'll be glad you did.

BE NICE TO EVERYONE

You've heard of six degrees of separation. I'm convinced if you know enough people, it's actually three degrees. It's a small world, so be nice to everyone you meet along the way. And I mean *everyone*. You never know when they may come back in to your life.

You never know whom they know. And think about this: You never know whom they know that you *want* to know. The person you met yesterday may end up opening a door for you to find your first job.

One Christmas Eve, two ladies walked into the lobby of a children's hospital and asked for the administrator in charge. He greeted them, gave them a tour of the hospital, and invited the women to join him for a cup of coffee. Even though he had several other things he needed to be doing, he made them feel that he had all the time in the world. As he walked the ladies to their car, they handed him a check for $100,000. The story doesn't end there.

About forty-five minutes later, the ladies returned and asked for the administrator. He greeted them again and invited the women to his office. They said, "No, thank you. We just visited another charity, where we were going to deliver our other $100,000 check. They said they were too busy and asked us to come back after the holidays. You were so nice to us earlier that we decided to give you the second check."

Be nice to everyone you meet. Something wonderful might happen.

THE MAGIC OF MENTORS

Why do you want a mentor? What impact can mentors make on your career? Think of a mentor as your trusted adviser. They are special people in your life whom you trust and respect. They'll give you advice and guidance. Mentors will show you the ropes and tell you what you need to hear, not necessarily what you want to hear. You'll have the opportunity to learn from their successes, as well as their mistakes.

I've been blessed with many mentors in my life. My first was my boss right out of college. Brenda Jackson took me under her wing. She was smart, thoughtful, and passionate. She had a strong work ethic and also knew how to have fun at work. I had the opportunity to work with Brenda for ten years. To this day, she's my mentor, my hero, and one of my best friends.

Other mentors I've had along the way have been people I admired and respected, and I just watched them in action. Some of the people I consider to be mentors don't even know it. Every relationship with a mentor is different. It may be a formal relationship, or it may be from afar.

If your company has a formal mentoring program, take advantage of the opportunity. Company-sponsored mentors are great because you're partnering with someone who can help you understand how that particular organization really works—formal and informal procedures, processes, and work culture.

Mentors make great sounding boards. Talking to them is a safe way for you to be frank and honest, while at the same time getting assessments of your progress and how you fit within the organization.

Also find a mentor (or two) outside your organization. Finding a mentor is relatively easy. Most people are honored when you ask for their thoughts, ideas, and advice. Is there someone who seems to be living the life to which you aspire? Ask the person to lunch. It could be the beginning of a wonderful relationship.

The best mentors not only help you in your professional life, they help you be a better person.

CHAPTER TEN

NEVER PASS UP A LEMONADE STAND

W hen you see a kid with a lemonade stand, do you stop because you're thirsty or because you want to make a child's day? Never pass up the opportunity to make someone's day. Find it in your heart to do something special every chance you get.

MAKE PEOPLE FEEL SPECIAL

Life is all about giving. When you give of yourself, you end up getting so much more in return. Always be thinking about what you can do to make someone else's day special.

One of the keys to building strong relationships is making people feel special. Go out of your way to let people know you appreciate them. Send them e-mails thanking them for their work on a project. Leave them voice mails thanking them for coming to your rescue when your printer wouldn't work. Consider doing something special when they least expect it.

Many years ago, I received the most beautiful floral arrangement I'd ever seen. I couldn't imagine who it was from. I opened the card and it read, "It's Nancy Barry Day at The Hotel Adolphus. From your friend, David Davis."

I was speechless. Why was my friend David Davis, director of public relations for The Adolphus, sending me flowers? We'd been friends for years, but it had been a long time since we'd spoken. My company had hosted some events at the hotel over the years, but we weren't working on any projects at the time. I called David to thank him and asked why in the world he had sent the flowers. He said, "When I woke up today, I was thinking about you, and I wanted you to have a special day."

WOW. When was the last time you did something like that for someone? Today is a great day to start.

There are so many easy ways to make people feel special. Send a note thanking them for their business. What if everyone in sales had to send a thank-you note before they received their commissions? What if you sent five handwritten notes a month, just because you wanted to make someone's day?

If you truly want someone to "feel the love," bring them food. Seriously, people will do *anything* for food. Think about it. You love it when someone brings something to eat. The whole place lights up. It's a great morale booster.

So, if you want to develop or strengthen your relationships internally or externally, you need to find a good chocolate chip cookie or cake recipe. Baking is like therapy for me. If it's not your thing, just buy something. They'll love you just the same.

I could tell you a million stories about magical things that have happened because I baked someone a cake or cookies. One time, I saved *The Dallas Morning News* $5,000 because I baked someone a double batch of chocolate chip cookies. We were planning an event on the field of Texas Stadium. The contract stated that we had to rent their plywood to put under the stage. It was going to cost $5,000. I said, "You have *got* to be kidding. Who owns the plywood?"

It was owned by concert producers in Houston. I thought for a minute, then said, "Let me make a few phone calls." It just so happened one of the guys in Houston used to work in Dallas and was a friend for whom I'd baked in the past. So I gave him a call. I hadn't talked to Scott in three years. He answered the phone, and I said, "Scott, it's Nancy Barry. I have the ultimate chocolate chip cookie deal for you." I explained the situation and told him if he would waive the $5,000 rental fee, I would bake him a double batch of chocolate chip cookies. He didn't even hesitate and said, "Done!"

Oh, the power of sweets. Oh, the power of relationships.

In addition to your clients, think about all the people at your company who help you be successful—especially the people behind the scenes whom we tend to forget. Do something special for them. What about the people in IT who come to your rescue when your computer has an attitude? Or the security guard who smiles at you every morning when you come to work? I used to take cinnamon butter cakes to our switchboard operators. They have a critical job at the company and are tucked away in a little office. You would have thought I'd just given them a huge raise.

It doesn't have to be something big. A handwritten note with something to eat, and you are bonded for life. It doesn't take much to make someone's day. Find your own special way to make others feel special.

THANK-YOU NOTES—A LOST ART

Do thank-you notes matter? One of the members of my twenty-somethings advisory board shared this experience with me. She had found her dream job. She went through the interviewing process and was one of two final candidates.

She wasn't offered the position. Through the interviewing process, she'd developed a good relationship with the hiring manager, so she decided to call to see why she wasn't selected. The woman explained that the only thing distinguishing her from the other leading candidate was a handwritten thank-you note the other one sent.

My friend had sent a thank-you note via e-mail, but the other candidate sent both an e-mail *and* a handwritten note. The bottom line: Thank-you notes matter. If you want to make a lasting impression, send a handwritten note.

Writing thank-you notes may sound like torture, but the more you do it, the easier it gets. It's easy to procrastinate when it comes to writing notes. One reason you may be putting it off is you feel you need to say something different in each note. Let me share some secrets with you.

First, chances are the only person who's going to read the note is the person you send it to, so you don't have to worry about being original in each note. Second, it's the thought that counts. People won't remember every word you wrote; what they'll remember is that you *sent* a note.

People want and need to feel appreciated. You need to find your special way to thank people. When you do, people will always remember you.

THE JOY OF GIVING BACK

You have so much to offer. You're young and smart. Share your time, energy, and talents to help make this world a better place.

There are so many nonprofit organizations that would benefit from your involvement. Identify something you are passionate about, and then do the research to find an organization addressing the issue. Volunteer to serve on a committee. Volunteer to help build houses. Volunteer to serve meals to the homeless.

I've had the opportunity to be involved in the community over the years, and it's been an amazing experience. Not only will your efforts benefit those in need, they will benefit you—personally and professionally.

You'll have the opportunity to meet some wonderful people. You'll develop relationships with people you might not have otherwise met. You will gain valuable experience and learn new skills. Chairing a committee could give you the experience you need to serve in a management role with your company.

One of the executives I surveyed for this book shares this story. "In my first couple of years out of college, I wasn't getting promoted as fast as I wanted. In addition to working hard and proving myself, I poured my energies into nonprofit leadership roles. I gained some valuable experience, managing several hundred people as we produced a very large community event. I had the opportunity to hone my leadership skills, which was noticed by the senior management of my company." Down the road, when it was time for a promotion, she had the experience her bosses were looking for.

Get involved in your community. Share your knowledge, talents, and gifts generously. Some of the best leadership training you can get is through volunteering.

CHAPTER ELEVEN

Random Words of Wisdom

◆

A Few More Things You Should Know

I've tried to shorten your learning curve with the information I covered in the previous chapters, but I have a few more things you should know. My friends and family would tell you that I have many random thoughts. I'll make a comment to my daughter, Lauren, and she'll smile and say, "That was random!" So, here's my list of random thoughts for you.

Be Able to Look in the Mirror and Ask, "Is It Me?"

Would you want to work with you? Be honest. Give yourself feedback. Is there something you're doing that needs improvement? Having the ability to look within is a tremendous asset.

If your co-workers are getting assigned the best projects and you're not, you should wonder why. Then do something about it. Do a self-performance review quarterly. Your goal will be to identify areas that need improvement and start improving them before someone has to ask you to.

Always Have Something to Write On.

Invest in a nice portfolio or small journal, and keep it with you at all times. How many times have you had a brilliant idea or thought of something you needed to do, and you didn't have anything to write on? Or you might be traveling with your boss in the car when he decides to give you all the details about a new project. You want to be prepared. Also, have a nice pen. Consider it an investment in your professional image.

Rise Above Office Politics.

You can run, but you can't hide, from office politics. Every organization is political to a certain extent. If you're frustrated with the politics in your office, don't think you can run to another organization to get away from them. My best advice: *Do not* get involved. Just focus on you and the great work you're doing.

Be Respectful of Other People's Time.

If you ask for thirty minutes, take twenty-nine. Whether the meeting is with a co-worker, your boss, or a client, be respectful of the other person's time. If you get on a roll and take an hour of their day, all they'll remember is you were the one who screwed up the rest of their day. If they say they want you to stay, great. If not, tell them you'll send them the rest of the information.

Representatives from a nonprofit organization once came to see me at *The Dallas Morning News*, seeking our support. They asked for thirty minutes on my calendar. When they arrived, they put an egg timer on my desk and set it for thirty minutes. They said, "We asked for thirty minutes, and when the timer goes off, we're leaving."

Sure enough, when the timer went off, they weren't through with their presentation. I told them I had extra time and they were welcome to stay. They smiled and said, "No, we asked for thirty minutes. We'll leave the rest of the presentation with you and call to follow up later."

I've *never* forgotten that meeting. While I don't suggest you take an egg timer with you into a meeting (it was a bit annoying listening to the tick-tick-tick the whole time), I do recommend you respect people's time.

Never Share Salary Information.

When you start your career, you may be tempted to tell your friends how much money you're making. Discussing salary is a no-win proposition. It just shouldn't be done.

There's a story of a young woman who was an accountant for a national nonprofit organization. She was working at one of their golf tournaments and met a man who was also an accountant. In the course of the conversation, she shared her salary information. What she didn't know was the man also knew her boss. He casually mentioned the conversation to her boss, and the employee was fired.

Be Observant.

You can learn a lot by just being observant. Observe the way the leaders of the company handle themselves in meetings or when dealing with difficult situations. If you observe the things around you, you'll be able to see when something needs to be done. Take the initiative before someone asks you to do it. Your management team doesn't have time to hold your hand. And their boss doesn't have time to hold their hands either.

Excuses, Excuses, Excuses.

Don't make excuses; just get your work done. Your manager doesn't want to hear why it's not done. She just needs to know when it *will* be done. Your manager will expect you to have an excuse. Surprise her and don't have one.

Create a "Pick Me Up" File.

Every time someone sends you a nice note, letter or e-mail, put a copy in your "pick me up" file. Then, on those days when you're being hard on yourself, wondering if you can do this job, read a couple of the notes people have sent you over the years. It'll remind you what a great job you are doing, and you'll have the renewed energy to keep going.

Be Willing.

Be willing to stay late, come in early, or skip lunch. Be willing to do whatever it takes to get the job done. Be willing to start at the bottom and work your way up. Almost everyone starts at the bottom. It's actually a good place to start. Be willing to get your hands dirty. Be willing to be the leader on one project and just a member of the team on the next one.

Times Change—It's a Fact of Life.

Bosses will change. Your responsibilities will change. The mission of your organization may change. It can be unsettling because of the fear of the unknown, but when something changes, embrace it, and go with the flow. The key is communicating any concerns you may have with your boss. And, it's important to know, sometimes change is the best thing that can happen.

What Does Your Heart Tell You to Do?

Sometimes it's best to follow your instincts. When you're trying to make a decision, do the necessary research. But in the end, your first instincts are the best answer. Your intuitions, those little voices in your head, are powerful.

Are You Thinking about Bringing Your Parents to Work?

There are stories about young professionals inviting their parents to sit in on their performance reviews, or to sit in on meetings when they're in trouble at work. Believe it or not, some parents are calling managers to complain about the amount of work their kids are being asked to do.

Promise me you won't bring your parents to a performance-related meeting, or let your parents call your boss. It's *your* responsibility to handle workplace issues. Your parents love you and can be a great resource. I encourage you to get their thoughts about issues at work, but leave it at that.

Try Not to Lose Your Cool in the Office.

If someone makes you mad, saying the first thing that comes to mind is probably not a good idea. If you feel as though you're going to lose your cool, walk away.

Wait a while before you say something. Depending how mad you are, you may need to wait a day or so. Give yourself some time to gather your thoughts and composure. There will be days when you'll want to scream at anyone who's nearby. Don't lose your cool.

There's No Room for Whining at Work.

Your college roommate may have put up with your whining, but your colleagues at work won't. I'm blown away by the number of adults who whine the way they did when they were four. There will be days when you're frustrated, but don't be a whiner.

Slow Down, You Move Too Fast—or Do You?

Every office is different. Some teams walk fast, talk fast, and move fast. Some teams are slower. You may need to adjust your speed. We had an intern one year who drove us crazy because she moved so slowly. We decided the next time we interviewed for the intern position, we would ask, "Do you walk fast, talk fast, and move fast?"

I'll be the first to admit that sometimes I talk too fast. Maybe it's because I'm from Texas. (Actually, that would explain the Southern accent while I'm talking fast.) When I realize I'm talking ninety miles per hour, I make a conscious effort to slow down. Think about your pace. Is it too fast? Too slow? If so, consider making the appropriate adjustments to accommodate others. Remember, it's all about them.

Just Say "Thank You."

How many times has someone paid you a compliment, and you quickly rejected it? When I was a senior in college, doing my student teaching at Nacogdoches High School, the teacher complimented me on the dress I was wearing. I went on and on about how old the dress was. After I *finally* finished telling her all the reasons why it wasn't a great dress, she looked at me and said, "All you had to say was 'thank you'."

She taught me a valuable lesson. When you reject a compliment, you're discounting the other person as well as yourself. The next time someone tries to pay you a compliment, bite your tongue, and enjoy the moment. Just smile and say "thank you."

Be the One Who Says "Hello."

I'm astounded by the number of people who walk through the hallways at work and never speak. They walk along staring at the floor. How boring is that? Be the one who smiles, looks people in the eye, and says "hello."

Go Easy on the Gum.

I love chewing gum. Perhaps you do too. If you're smacking away and someone walks in your office to talk about a big project, what are you going to do with the gum? What if you're on the way to a meeting and you forget to take the gum out of your mouth before you go in? I'm not suggesting you give up chewing gum, just be careful when and where you chew it.

When I worked at the TV station, there was a woman who went on the morning show with gum in her mouth. No one noticed it until it was too late. She was on the air (live!), chewing her gum through the entire interview. Think about her before you walk into your next client meeting.

Never Trash Your Employer.

I am stunned by the number of people, young and old, who speak poorly of their employers. You may not agree with everything that happens at your organization, but remember we're all on the same team. (Not to mention, your employer puts food on your table.)

And there are so many people who send e-mails, from their work addresses, to family and friends about how they hate their jobs and their bosses. What are they thinking? Remember, those e-mails are *not* private conversations. Your employer can find them. If that happens, you're toast.

The next time someone asks, "How's your job?" if you can't think of one positive thing to say, it may be time to move on to your next career opportunity.

Never Answer Your Cell Phone in a Public Restroom.

Trust me, I know. I'd had a crazy morning at the office and had run out the door to a lunch meeting. When I arrived at the restaurant, I ran to the ladies' room. While I was in there, my cell phone rang. It was someone from the TV station. I didn't think the call would take long, so I answered it.

What I didn't realize was that I was in a stall with the automatic flush feature. I'm sure you know what happened next. I learned a valuable lesson. No matter who is calling, a restroom is not the place for a phone conversation.

Getting Caught Up in the Grapevine Is Not in Your Best Interest.

Office gossip is dangerous. Some days you may think your office is a soap opera or reality show. Make sure you're not the star of the show. Stay out of the grapevine. Gossiping about employees or company business can get you in trouble—big trouble.

If someone wants to gossip, politely say you're not interested. When people gossip, two careers are at risk—that of the person being talked about and that of the person doing the talking. Don't go there.

Love Is in the (Office) Air.

You've been invited to a meeting with another department. You see someone across the room who catches your attention. There's something special about him or her, and you start daydreaming about your first date.

Before you dream too much, think about this: How often do office romances work? When and if it ends, what will your life be like? Will you be peering around corners to make sure your former love is not in the hall? Will it be awkward if you're in a meeting together? And if the relationship ends on a bad note, will one party run to human resources to file a harassment claim?

I am *not* a "date doctor." I just want you to think about the potential consequences before an office romance begins. If there's no way to stop it, one of you might need to consider finding a new job.

Make It Look Easy, but Not Too Easy.

You want to be known as someone who makes it happen, without ever complaining about the workload. However, if you make it look too easy, your boss won't have a clue how much work you're doing.

When I made the decision to leave the corporate world, I realized my bosses didn't really know everything I handled for the company. Why didn't they know? Because I never told them. I didn't want anything to fall through the cracks when I left, so I prepared a detailed, three-page list of my job responsibilities. When I presented it to one of my bosses, he smiled and said, "This will be helpful!"

It's your job to make it look easy, but you also want to be sure the management team knows how much you're doing. Consider sending your boss a quarterly update on your accomplishments. It'll help her know what's going on, and it will give her useful information when it's time for your annual performance review. But don't make it look like it's all about you. Share the credit. Compliment your colleagues involved in your successes.

Learn When (and How) to Say "No."

It took me a long, long time to learn how to say "no." Early in my career, I didn't want to say "no" to anything. I didn't want to miss an opportunity to do something new, learn something new, or meet someone new.

I'm still not very good at it, but I've learned through the years that it's sometimes better to say "no." If you can't give a new project your best, it may be better to decline the opportunity.

If your boss asks you to take on another project, and you're already swamped, you might be tempted to say, "Are you crazy? You want me to add this to my plate? There's no way."

Resist the urge to say what you're really thinking. Instead, say something like, "I would love to have the opportunity to work on that project, but I'm not sure I could do that and complete all the other projects I'm working on. I need your help to prioritize the things I'm responsible for right now."

Put yourself in your boss' shoes. There's no way he can keep up with all the things you've been asked to do. He just knows you're really good, and he wants you to work on this project. Don't immediately think he's trying to kill you with extra work. Work with your boss to determine if there's time to add this new opportunity to your list.

Sometimes we have to be willing to say "no" to some things, so we can say "yes" to other opportunities that come our way. Learning to say "no" takes practice. Give it some time, and you'll master the art of doing it graciously and professionally.

Be Careful What You Do on Your Own Time.

This one falls into the category of things you need to hear, not necessarily what you want to hear. You represent your organization twenty-four hours a day, seven days a week. Does this mean they own you? Not necessarily, but sort of. Every move you make and every word you speak reflects on your organization, as well as on you.

Know When to Aim High and When to Aim Low.

If you're introducing someone and can't remember her title, aim high. If you're not sure if she is a manager, director, or vice president, it's better to go with the higher title. It'll avoid an embarrassing situation and it'll make the person feel good.

If you're dining at a business function, aim low when ordering. Don't get something more expensive than your host's choice. If you're debating whether to order another glass of wine, aim low—real low. Consider saying, "No, thank you." You never want to put yourself in a situation where you have too much to drink at business functions.

If someone asks how old you think she is, don't go there. But if you have to, aim low. When you're tipping someone for services, aim high. Would you want to park a car in the rain and get tipped a dollar? Be generous.

I have a special place in my heart for waiters and waitresses who serve breakfast. The total bill isn't typically much, so if you just tip fifteen percent, the waitress may walk away with less than a dollar for serving you for an hour. Kick in an extra buck.

Never Underestimate the Power of a Secretary.

I'm convinced most companies are run by secretaries. Be their friend and they will be yours. They have the ears of the big bosses;

don't ever forget that. If they like you, they'll tell their bosses. If they don't like you, they'll tell their bosses.

A lot can be learned from how people treat secretaries and receptionists. Employers feel it can be an accurate reflection of how candidates would treat their co-workers and clients. Keep that in mind when you're interviewing for a job.

Secretaries are among the most important people in any organization, and should be treated with respect. They hold the key to the door you want opened. They actually hold the key to everything.

Play by the Rules, Even If No One Told You What the Rules Are.

There are written rules and unwritten rules. It's your responsibility to follow all of them. Your employer can't have rules for everything, so use your common sense. If your manager doesn't go over the policies and procedures, ask if there's a document you can review. If they give you an employee handbook, take time to read it. Most employees just put it in the desk. There's no telling what you might learn, if you take the time to read it.

Keep Your Car Clean.

What if your boss called you right now and asked you to take him to the airport? What would you do? Panic? Your car says a lot about you. Keep it clean, especially if you're in a position where you call on clients.

Don't keep junk in the trunk. Someone may need to put a box or suitcase back there. If someone opens your trunk, and it looks like you live out of it, you're going to be embarrassed. Also, keep your car filled with gas. You don't want to run out of gas on the way to an important meeting.

Always Carry Some Cash.

I can feel it. The mom in me is coming out. Always keep cash with you. You never know when might need it. What if there's an emergency? What if you take a client to lunch and have to pay for the valet? Do you really want to have to borrow the money from your client?

CHAPTER TWELVE

DOWN THE ROAD

———— ◆ ————

I n chapter 7, I talked about the need to have a plan and the need
to set realistic expectations. It's important to realize you may not
be able to move as fast as you'd like in your career. Be patient. If
you move too fast, you'll miss some important experiences that will
help you later.

After you've been in your position for awhile, you may begin to
think you're ready to move on to something else. You may be hoping
for a promotion within your organization, or you may decide you
want to move on to something different.

PREPARING FOR A PROMOTION

If one of your goals is to move up the ladder, start preparing now.
You want to do everything you can to position yourself as the best
candidate for a promotion down the road.

Choose the position you want next, then develop a plan to
acquire the skills and traits you'll need for the job. If you have your

eye on a position in another department, start building relationships with key decision makers. You want them to know you before a new job opportunity comes along.

Be careful what you wish for. Just because you love what you're doing now doesn't mean you'll love being a manager. Do some research about the position you have your eye on, so you can be sure it's really what you want.

When You're the Boss

If your promotion involves managing a team, go back and re-read chapter 8, "Bosses: The Good, the Bad, and the Ugly." Don't assume you'll know how to do everything, because you won't. How could you? Sure, some of it is common sense, but a lot of the skills you'll need to be a good manager will have to be learned.

Ask to go to a training class. If your organization doesn't offer management training, find a training class on your own. Go to a continuing education class at your local university. Sign up for a seminar offered by an outside organization. Go to the bookstore and find a book for first-time managers. Do whatever it takes to be sure you have the tools you need to be a great boss and succeed in your new role.

Being promoted is exciting, but there are challenges that come with it. If you're promoted within your current department, you'll now be supervising people who were your peers before. Be prepared for some awkward moments. It will take time to *earn* their trust and respect.

And be sensitive to your colleagues who may have also applied for the position. Sit down with them to discuss any concerns they may have. Create an environment where your new team feels comfortable sharing thoughts, ideas, and concerns with you.

When you're part of management, you'll need to step everything up a notch—your attire, professional image, communication skills, and ability to work with the team. And you'll want to make it a priority to build and nurture relationships with other managers. Remember, we're all on the same team.

What If You Don't Get the Promotion?

Give yourself twenty-four hours to deal with it. Being upset isn't going to change anything. Going to your boss and losing your temper isn't going to change the decision.

If you rant and rave to anyone in the office who will listen, it will get back to your boss. How would you feel about promoting someone who acted like that? It would probably confirm why you didn't get the promotion in the first place. There was a gentleman who was a star performer, but he didn't receive the promotion he thought he deserved. He went around the office bashing his boss for making such a poor decision. Even though he was one of the firm's top performers, he ended up getting fired.

Focus on what you need to do to get the next promotion. There's a reason you didn't get this one. You don't know all the reasons someone else was chosen. You may never know. You can't change the decision, so why waste your mental energy? Use your energy instead to focus on what you need to do now.

After you cool off, consider having a conversation with your boss that goes something like this. "Susan, I have to tell you I was disappointed I didn't get the promotion. I realize a lot of factors went into your decision, and I will support your decision to promote Marty. I'd love for you to tell me what I can do to prepare for the next opportunity."

You didn't attack, and you were calm. You didn't question your boss's decision. And you made it easy for her to tell you what you can do moving forward. You've done everything you can do. Now it's time to let it go. Focus on getting ready for the next opportunity.

IS IT TIME TO MOVE ON?

At some point along your journey, you may decide it's time to move on to a different organization. Perhaps you'll decide the career you chose right out of college isn't for you.

Before you make a change, I have some things I'd like you to consider. You're the only one who can answer these questions. It's your life. It's your career. I just want to share what I'd be asking you if we were in a coaching session.

I encourage you not to make a career decision if your emotions are extremely high or low. Talk to people you trust. What does your heart tell you to do? If you don't have peace about moving on, don't do it until you do. The grass isn't always greener on the other side. *It's still grass.*

Your career will be filled with ups and downs. Just because you have one bad day doesn't mean it's time to jump ship. Give it time. Hang in there. The reality is you're going to have bad days.

There will be days when you're on top of the world, where you love your job—the people, the projects—all of it. Then there will be days when you think you can't do this *one* more day. On those days when you start thinking it may be time to move on, step back, and look at the big picture. What was it that sent you over the edge? What did you love about your job yesterday? Have a conversation with your boss. Ask where you stand. Ask for candid feedback on your career opportunities.

Many times, people leave their jobs because they don't like their bosses. If you love the work you're doing and you love the other people, is it *really* worth leaving because of your boss? Have you done everything within your power to build a relationship with your boss? What if your boss leaves right after you do? Will you wish you had stayed? Picture yourself leaving your position. Are you sure you want to start all over?

Have you looked at opportunities in other departments at your company? If you love the organization, why leave? If you see another department you're interested in, find out who heads it, and set up a time to meet. Tell him you'd like to have the opportunity to know more about what they do. Who knows, you may have a found a new career. At the very least, you've developed a new relationship with another colleague.

Is it about the money? You have bills to pay and dreams you want to save for, but the money won't matter if you're not happy. Picture yourself in a position where you're making more, but you can't stand the job or the people you work with. If you end up in a position where you work all the time and don't like what you're doing, will the money be worth it? You're the only one who knows the answer.

Never underestimate the value of your benefits. Before moving on to another organization, ask about the benefits. Compare them, line by line, with your current package. There are so many people who take their benefits for granted. All we focus on is our base salary, because after all, that's what we're living on.

I always knew my benefit package was good, but I didn't have a full appreciation for it until I left to start my own business. I walked away from medical benefits, a 401(K) match, and life insurance. I did extensive research before I made the decision to leave, and I encourage you to do the same. The value of my benefits obviously didn't stop me from making the change, but it gets your attention when you realize how much they are worth.

Make a list of the pros and cons of moving on. What will you gain by changing jobs? What will you give up? What do you love about your current position? What can't you stand? What do you love about the people you work with? Will your new position require you to move? Will the hours be better or worse? Is the career path with the new opportunity better than what you have now? Are you sure?

Review the list over and over until you're comfortable with your decision. Review the list with people you trust and respect. Ask them to give you their candid feedback. And ask them to keep the conversation confidential. When I was thinking about walking away from the best job in the world to start my own business, I met with five of my mentors. I asked each of them to tell me what I *needed* to hear, not what I *wanted* to hear. I encourage you to do the same.

If you think switching jobs is the fastest way to get to the top, think again. You might not like the consequences. Employers may be leery of people who hop from one job to another every couple of years. They may wonder why you can't stay put. Is it because you get restless? It is because you can't get along with co-workers, or do you keep getting asked to leave?

Over the years, as I've reviewed resumes for open positions, I carefully review how long the candidate has been in previous positions. If the candidate has ten years experience but has changed jobs every twelve to eighteen months, I rarely give them serious consideration.

Put yourself in the shoes of the prospective employers. They're going to spend a tremendous amount of time, money, and energy training you. It could take years before you've learned everything they want you to know. It's not in the company's best interest to hire someone who will probably leave after a short time.

It's difficult to juggle looking for a job with holding down a job. While it's easier to get a job when you have a job, don't job hunt while you're at work. Use your evenings and weekends to do the research. Take vacation time if you have to.

The last thing you want is for your current employer find out you're looking for a job on his dime. Remember, your employer can track your e-mails and the Web sites you visit. If you're not careful, you may be looking for a new job earlier than you planned.

If You Decide to Move On

Once you make a decision to move on, don't second-guess yourself. Move forward with a positive attitude. Here are a few tips to keep in mind as you're moving on.

In a perfect world, you want to leave while they still love you. At the very least, you want to leave on good terms. Never, ever burn a bridge. You may need that bridge one day. You may decide you want to come back one day. The grass might not be greener on the other side.

Prepare a letter of resignation and schedule time to meet with your manager. Don't just leave it on her desk. The letter should be short and sweet. Thank the company for the time you spent there. Resist the urge to say anything negative—always take the high road.

What if your boss makes a counteroffer? What if she offers to match your new salary, or beat it? What if you're offered a promotion? These questions will help you get to the bottom of why you're really leaving. Was it about the money? Was it about your career path? Just be prepared for the conversation.

Don't leave them hanging. Give at least two weeks' notice. Brief your colleagues on pending projects. Make sure your files are organized, so they can find everything after you're gone.

The last piece of advice I'll share with you is to take some time off between jobs. I'd been at the same company for ten years when *The Dallas Morning News* recruited me to join their company. They were anxious for me to start immediately. I gave my former employer two weeks' notice, but didn't take any time off between jobs. Oh, how I wished I had. Give yourself time to rest and get caught up in other areas of your life.

Changing jobs may seem like a great idea, until you think about all it entails. Be sure you're making a decision that's best for your long term success.

As you begin your new journey, remember it takes about ninety days to get back in your comfort zone. During that time, you may wonder *what* you were thinking when you left your other job. Give it some time. The best is yet to come.

A FINAL MESSAGE FROM YOUR NEW CAREER COACH

---◆---

Thank you for taking the time to read this book. Thanks to you, I have a dream job. I hope you've found yours, too. If you haven't found it quite yet, you will. Keep believing. Keep your dreams alive.

My ultimate goal while writing this book was to share information that will help you be successful. I hope you enjoyed reading the book as much as I enjoyed writing it. Would you do me a favor? I'd love to hear your thoughts about *When Reality Hits*. What was the most helpful part? Tell me what's missing, so I can make the next edition even better. Please e-mail your comments, thoughts, and ideas to: nancy@nancybarry.com.

So, what are you going to do now? You're going to enjoy every precious moment of your career. You're going to hold your head high with a tremendous amount of pride.

I want you to look in the mirror and see what others see: an amazing person who chose to get a great education. Someone who will make a difference in this world—someone who has chosen to leave a legacy.

You're going to walk through life with a smile on your face and a sparkle in your eye. You've going to have a positive attitude and see everything as an opportunity. Let people see and feel your passion for life, and when you do, you can sit back and watch the magic unfold. May all your dreams come true.

Wishing you the best—always!

Nancy Barry

INDEX

BIOGRAPHY

N ancy Barry is a motivational speaker and author who has a passion for helping recent college graduates succeed in their careers. She has spoken to thousands of young professionals helping them understand the importance of "soft skills" in the workplace. Nancy shares her extensive business experience to shorten the learning curve for twentysomethings entering the workforce.

Prior to starting her own company, Nancy spent twenty-five years in the corporate world. For the last sixteen years of her career, Nancy worked for *The Dallas Morning News* and WFAA-TV, where she served as Vice President of Community Services and Vice President for The Dallas Morning News Charities, an annual campaign that raises money for the hungry and homeless.

Nancy is a member of numerous professional organizations, including the National Speakers Association and the National Association of Colleges and Employers. She is also very involved in her community serving on various boards and committees, including the advisory councils of the Communities Foundation of Texas and Dallas Women's Foundation.

She earned her Bachelor of Science degree from Stephen F. Austin State University. Nancy lives in Dallas, Texas, and is the proud mother of two children, Chris and Lauren.

If you would like to invite Nancy to speak to your group, please contact her at: www.nancybarry.com.